TOUGH KID

THE LIFE AND FILMS OF

FRANKIE DARRO

BY

JOHN GLOSKE

**DEDICATED TO
STEVE MONZO
"I'm still laughing."**

"They were wrong to take us children and do that with our lives, to twist our environment in that way and then leave it for us to sort out."

Roddy McDowell

TABLE OF CONTENTS

CHAPTER 1
WHO WAS FRANKIE DARRO?

To paraphrase a political debate of some years ago, "I knew Frankie Darro, I worked with Frankie Darro (well sort of), Frankie Darro was a friend of mine..." Well you may know the rest. Most young actors today are no Frankie Darro, but then most young actors-or the general public for that matter-have never heard of Frankie Darro. So, who was he?

Frankie Darro was one of the most prolific actors of his generation. His career spanned from roles in silent movies through a myriad of starring roles in "B" movies and serials and supporting roles in major A films and eventually television. Frankie appeared on screen with a virtual who's who of stars of the Golden Age of Hollywood, including Clark Gable, Jean Harlow, the Marx Brothers, James Cagney, and on and on.

Towards the end of his short life Frankie had befriended me and my friend Steve Monzo not long after my eighteenth birthday. Although we remained friends for the final four years of his life, Frankie died before I was able to view some of his best work. I knew of his films mainly from the very few that would pop up on Saturday morning television or some occasional late night showing.

Upon moving to Los Angeles a few years after his death, I decided to do some research on my late friend. I scoured the research libraries and came up with virtually nothing. The information that was available always seemed to be the same paragraphs, just written in different ways.

With the advent of home video in the early 1980's I started collecting his films. After watching and re-watching these decades of old movies, I was constantly amazed by his performances. Even if the plot and everyone else in the film were dull and tired, Frankie would seem to shine. Whether he was the good guy or the tough kid who eventually turned around to be the good guy, Frankie was always eminently watchable.

As time marched on and film books on every subject imaginable began to line book store shelves everywhere, there was still little of note regarding Frankie.

I decided to tell his story for one reason. It's my hope that when someone sees Frankie in a film and they are so inclined to find out a little more about his life and films, there would be at least one source available.

It is my hope that this book will at least partially answer the question, "Who was Frankie Darro?"

CHAPTER 2
THE FLYING JOHNSONS

During the later part of the nineteenth century the Sells Brothers Circus was second in success only to The Ringling Brothers Circus. To drive the point home, one of their advertising posters exclaimed, "Sells Brothers World Conquering And All Overshadowing Three Ring Circus, Real Roman Hippodrome, Indian Village, and Pawnee Bill's Famous Wild West Show." Circuses were not known for selling themselves short.

With the death of brother Ephrain Sells in 1898 half of the business interest was sold off to competing circuses. A few years later in 1905 Lewis Sells, the sole brother remaining in the business, sold off his shares completely.

By 1906, the circus was renamed Sells-Floto Circus and was owned by Harry Tannen and Fred Bonfils. The circus continued to crisscross the country, carefully avoiding the areas that were dominated by the Ringling Brothers. The Sells-Floto Circus traveled by train, a rarity among circuses at the time, as most traveled by trucks and cars. At the height of their popularity the circus employed three hundred and twenty-two workers, sixty performers, and a myriad of wild animals living in some fifty secure cages. The circus also employed an aerial act that performed under the name of The Flying Johnsons. The act consisted of Frank Johnson, born in 1887 at Eureka, California, and his wife Ada, who was born Ada Seigest in the Mediterranean seaport of Nice, France. Also in the act was a fellow by the name of Giovanni. The act was performed on the high trapeze, with Giovanni helping Frank with the mid-air transfers and catches for Ada. For up to three shows a day Ada put her life on the line by being tossed into the air, far above the circus tent's floor, and then caught by one of the two men in her life.

Criss crossing the country on a circus train was a difficult way to make a living in 1917. The quarters were cramped and unsanitary. Privacy was scarce for the Flying Johnsons.

Affairs and out of wedlock births were a common occurrence on the train. These were not ideal living conditions for anyone, especially for someone like Ada, who was not emotionally stable. Little by little Ada was starting to feel the strain of performing. Her nerves were beginning to fray, not a good sign for an aerialist. Being an integral part of the act and married to Frank, quitting was not an option. Without her, Frank and Giovanni would not have an act. Ada's health dilemma was solved, for the time being away, when during the month of April 1917 she discovered she was pregnant.

It's not clear who exactly the father was. Giovanni had apparently been involved with Ada prior to her pregnancy, but it could have also been her husband's child inside her. She might not even have known herself. What is known is that on December 17, 1917 during a blizzard in Chicago, she gave birth to a baby boy, whom they christened Frank Johnson, Jr. It's also not exactly clear what the Johnsons were doing in Chicago at the time of Frank Jr.'s birth. It's been written that they were on a tour stop with the circus. However the circus usually wrapped up its season in December touring the southern states. Chicago was much too cold for outdoor performing, as all the performances were done under the big top.

Soon after his birth Frank Jr., now known as Frankie, would be tended by one of the many circus performers while his mom and dad and Giovanni made their way up to the high wire, and with a swing of the trapeze, the Flying Johnsons were back in business.

As soon as Frankie was able to walk, Frank Sr. started to train his son in the art of aerialism. But there was a problem for the new father, one difficult to imagine for someone accustomed to spending his working hours swinging from a trapeze. From the very beginning Frankie was frightened of heights. He would scream and cry as his father climbed up the ladder to the trapeze. Frank Sr. perplexed by the dilemma, finally came up with the solution. He would stretch some wire low to the ground between two poles. Frankie was placed on the wire and taught the proper method of balance, and eventually he was taught to walk on the low lying wire. Once little Frankie had mastered the task, Frank Sr. adjusted the wire farther off the ground. With his confidence building, Frankie's fear of heights disappeared. Other circus performers aided with his education. They taught Frankie how to do back flips, head spins and juggling.

Early Portrait.

As soon as he was able to talk coherently, Frankie was added to the act. After Frank and Ada had performed their act, little Frankie would trot out in front of the audience and yell, "My father thanks you from the bottom of his heart, my mother thanks you from the bottom of her heart, and me, I thank you from my bottom too!" The speech would never fail to bring down the house. Frankie also learned a two-minute dance routine that would terminate in a triple head spin, another routine that would always delight the audiences. Frankie would appear with his parents, except on the rare occasions when the local authorities would not grant Frankie a work permit.

With Frankie now part of the act, Ada's nerves again felt the strain of performing. She knew that it was her responsibility to hold up her part of the act, but try as she might, the stress was starting to consume her.

In 1922 The Flying Johnsons were appearing in the coastal community of Long Beach, California. Ada's nerves, which were strained for much too long, finally snapped, and she suffered a nervous breakdown. Frank had her committed to a local hospital, and now with Ada out of the picture and Giovanni long gone, he would have to figure a way to support his family. One Flying Johnson did not an act make.

With Hollywood less than twenty-five miles to the north, Frank figured he could take a crack at the movie business. He was still in great shape, athletic and lean, and since he was already in show business, he felt he might as well give it a shot. He left Ada in the care of the hospital and took his four and a half year old son to Hollywood.

Sadly, Ada would never be a part of their lives again. Whether Frank officially filed for divorce is not known, but Frank took over complete care of Frankie, and he did this knowing that Frankie just might not be his own son.

Hollywood in the early 1920's was a dusty small town that was being rapidly populated by people from all parts of the world trying to make a buck from the burgeoning film industry. It wasn't difficult for someone with stamina and a little talent to at least grab a low rung job in the movies. Gower Gulch, a so-called slum section of Gower and Sunset Blvd., was known for its fly by night studios, which specialized in churning out quickie westerns.

The streets were populated by ex-cowboys, roustabouts and even circus folks looking for jobs as on-screen cowboys, extras or even stunt men. Frank fit right in, and before long he was working regularly as a stunt man, making enough money to support himself and his son. Frank even took up professional boxing, fighting in the bantam weight class, in order to bring home money to support the two of them. Frank found an apartment in Hollywood close to most of the studios. On the days he was not working he would continue to train Frankie in the fine art of circus performing. It was the only trade he knew, and he was determined to pass his skills on to his son. To earn extra money they would also perform an act in the vaudeville houses around town. Frankie was an immediate hit with the audiences.

It surprised Frank just how well his son took to performing, it dawned on him that his son just might be talented enough to have a crack at the movies himself. Three years earlier in 1921 Charlie Chaplin had released his film, *The Kid.* The film is now widely regarded as a classic and made a star out of seven year old Jackie Coogan. After the success of the film, the flood gates opened for child actors. Movie theatres were inundated with films featuring precocious kids, usually in some sort of peril. Storefronts throughout Hollywood sprang up with small time drama and dance teachers offering to train children for future movie stardom. Parents from across the country were convinced that their offspring could and would be the next Jackie Coogan. They grabbed their child, or in some cases children, headed west before their prodigy grew out of their precociousness.

Frank had worked for the former actor Ralph Ince, now a popular director. Ince was the youngest of three brothers who were also active in the film industry, they included John and the ill-fated Thomas. Frank figured that Ince would be the best person to approach about his talented son. Unfortunately Ince was overwhelmed with requests from parents about their talented offspring and refused to see Frankie. Undeterred, Frank had a follow up plan.

He knew Ince by sight and could see his office from behind the studio fence. With his son in tow he decided to wait behind the fence for Ince to emerge from his office. When the director finally emerged from his office, Frank boosted five year old Frankie up on the fence, and in a flash Frankie was up and over the temporary obstacle. Frankie ran right up to Ince, and before the studio guards could catch up with him, he performed one of his well rehearsed back flips and head spins.

The guards finally caught up with him and grabbed him away from the stunned director, but Ince was impressed enough and called the officers off. "Let's put this kid in a movie," he supposedly said. Standing on the outside looking in Frank smiled. His plan had worked. Ince did not have a role for Frankie in any of his current projects, but he did find a spot for him in fellow director Del Andrews' latest film, *Judgment of the Storm.* A family drama, the film was written by a Pittsburgh housewife named of E.S. Middleton and the film starred Ralph Hughes and Lucille Rickson. Rickson portrayed Mary Heath, and Frankie was cast as one of her twin children, with the other played by Fay McKenzie.

Variety, the popular trade publication enjoyed the film, said it was better than the majority of films playing in the first run houses and that with a few changes it could have been an outstanding film.

CHAPTER 3
THE SILENT YEARS

Frank Johnson, Sr. had hit the jackpot and pulled the brass ring all on the same day, without even realizing it. He had no way of knowing that due to his son's impromptu meeting with Ralph Ince, he would never climb the high wire again. His now six year old son would be the bread winner from now on.

Frank Sr. wasted no time in finding young Frankie additional work after his film debut, and he found Frankie the work all by himself, no agents for him! He would handle all of Frankie's business dealings himself. Why cut into the profits? He knew show business as well as anyone. If he could sell himself as a stuntman surely he could sell Frankie as the next in demand child star. Frank Sr. placed ads in the various trade publications touting the fact that if you wanted Frankie, you were to call Frank Sr. direct. The ad read "No Agent."

Frank had always been a stern task master and was not about to let any studio get the better of him when it was time to negotiate a deal on Frankie.

Reassessing Frankie's silent film career is a difficult task. 85-90% of all silent films are considered lost. The percentage is even greater for the late silent period between 1925 and 1929. With the advent of talking pictures between 1927 and 1928, theater owners rushed to equip their cinemas with sound. Some rural theaters hung in a bit longer, but the silent films died a rather swift death. Almost overnight they were considered antiques, a product of a bygone era. To add to their demise, anyone with a print of a silent movie could sell it off for its silver content. The print was destroyed in the process, but the owner of the print was left with some ready cash for his effort.

Frankie appeared in at least fifty-eight silent films between the years of 1923 and 1929. Sadly, only six are known to exist as of this writing. The earliest of his surviving films is the 1924 Universal-Jewel production of *Signal Tower*. The sixty-five minute movie stars Virginia Valli, Rickliff Fellows and future MGM star Wallace Beery. Frankie plays the child of a happily married couple who live in a secluded mountain area. Fellows (who plays Frankie's father David) works at the railroad signal tower nearby. A fellow railroad worker has been replaced by a man with a reputation for chasing women, well played by Beery. Without a close place to live, Beery moves in with the family. Needing a companion, David fixes him up with his wife's sister, but it's David's wife he's really after. At the showdown, Berry is about to rape David's wife, until David goes after him with what he believes is an empty gun. Unbeknown to David, his son (played by Frankie) has loaded a round in the revolver's chamber. The loaded gun quickly brings justice to the tense scene. The film is suspenseful throughout. A sense of coming dread hangs over the entire film, which makes it still entertaining over seventy years after its initial release. Adding to the film's realism is the fact the film was shot on location at Fort Bragg California, using the Skunk Works Railroad that was still operational until recently.

Frankie at age seven is a delight. He performs a stunt when a train engineer tosses him from the train's engine compartment, and into the waiting arms of his father. There is also a cute gag when his father steals a piece of chocolate cake and blames the missing cake on his son. Frankie's comic reaction shows him to be a natural comic performer with the ability to show pathos at a drop of the hat.

Frankie was no mere child performer, in comparison with the mentioned hoards descending on Hollywood during the 1920's Frankie was a natural, a talented performer who his father thought, might just have a shot at stardom. Even the popular trade paper *Varity* took note of Frankie's performance in *Signal Tower*, stating in its review, "A clever child study comes from Frankie Darro."

That same year found Frankie in another film built around a railroad. In *Roaring Rails*, starring the popular western star Harry Carey, the outdoor adventure story concerns a railroad and the efforts to restore sight to a blind boy (played by Frankie). For his efforts Frankie again received a glowing review from *Variety*, "The little boy [Darro] is not only a likable kid in the picture, but he was well coached. To see him cry when his 'Pop' was about to send him away to board was well worth watching." The newspaper ads for the movie billed Frankie as the screens "Wonder child". Frankie and Carey would team up again during the early days of sound films. With Frankie making money as an actor there was little need for Frank Sr. to look for employment of his own again. Besides, he was in his mid 30's at this time and going back up on the high wire, or doing stunt was not as appealing as it had been just a few years earlier when he was younger and hungry. Since Frankie had been in demand from the beginning Frank was able to ask for more and more money for his son's acting. The money Frankie made was spent on a nice home, a luxury car, and other niceties that an ex-circus performer could only dream of. The home Senior purchased for them was fondly remembered by Frankie. Frankie had spent his young life moving from one hotel room or apartment to another. At least for the time being Frankie had someplace to call a home. However, no thought was ever given to tomorrow, no thought of saving something or the proverbially rainy day. Unfortunately, these lessons taught to Frankie at such a young age were carried with him for the rest of his life. This was well before the Coogan law took effect protecting the wages of child performers. Before the law, the parents or guardians simply spent the money as they saw fit, leaving many child performers penniless as their careers came to an end. Once the Coogan law was passed, a percentage of a child performer's salary was put into a trust fund, to be opened once the child turned twenty-one. Since this was the mid 20's, Frankie's money all belonged to dad.

Besides money, there was also the question of education. Few show business people at the time gave thought to formal education. Frank Sr. had done all right without much education, and besides, how much education did little Frankie need? On screen he was a natural. "Just keep him working" was the slogan of the day.

Frankie did attend school, of course, but more often than not he was pulled out of class to go to the studio or on to location somewhere. There was supposed to be a teacher on the set, but when you're making a movie, there are higher priorities. Just keep the kid working.

With Frankie's rapid rise in fame and money a name from out of the past reentered their lives. Frankie's mother Ada had seen Frankie's rise to fame also and now wanted a piece of the action. She would initiate court action against her ex-husband for what she felt was her share of the money that Frankie was earning. The fight over Frankie's earnings would drag on for years.

On January 18, 1925 Frankie appeared in the sixty minute programmer *Women and Gold* starring Frank Mayo. Frankie was billed as Darrow in the credits. This would occasionally happen on his silent films. It was simply a mistake and not an effort to change his name.

Only two years after making his screen debut Frankie was tapped for an important role at Metro-Goldwyn Pictures. The film was *Confessions of a Queen.* The film was directed by Victor Seastrom, fresh off the Lon Chaney classic *He Who Gets Slapped.*

In the film Frankie plays Prince Zara, the offspring of the king and queen of a small and decadent empire named Illyria. The king (played by Lewis Stone) causes such furor over his hedonistic lifestyle that he is forced to abdicate. He finally winds up in Paris and finds happiness by living incognito with his wife and child.

The film was a major release for Metro. Its press notes called the film "The most important event in Seastrom's career." But then again they also announced boldly that Frankie was "a descendant of a royal family in Europe."

In a push to publicize his talented son, Frank Sr. had the world famous boxer Jack Dempsey pose for some pictures with Frankie. One photo that made it into the newspaper claimed that Frankie was the champ's favorite second when he was working out in Los Angeles. It must have made Frank Sr., an ex-boxer very proud to have the champ pose with his son.

Perhaps the most frustrating aspect of Frankie's silent period are the missing films he appeared in with cowboy star Tom Tyler. Between the years 1925 and 1929, Tyler and Frankie appeared in an amazing twenty-six western films together. Frankie's ability on horse back in the series earned him the nickname "Midget Cowboy". His costar Tyler born with the less than western name of Vincent Markowski in Port Henry, New York in 1902 or 1903 depending on the source. Tyler was a much in demand western star by the mid 1920's. Unfortunately, out of twenty-six films they appeared in together, only one seems to have survived. That film is the 1928 release of *Texas Tornado*.

Frankie would play different characters in the series, but in this entry he plays Buddy Martin, an orphan living with a woman and her father on a ranch where they hope to strike oil. The bank is about to foreclose on their ranch when a good natured stranger, played by Tyler, saves the day as he mounts his horse, rides off in a flash and arrives at the bank just in the nick of time to renew the lease. Later, Tyler is accused of beating the owner of the ranch into a coma and now must clear his good name. He not only clears his name, he falls in love with the woman who has cared for Frankie, and in the final seconds admits to Frankie that he is his long lost Uncle Tom. Tom gives Frankie a warm hug as the film fades out. It is easy to see why the series was so popular. It's full of fistfights, horse riding action and pathos, featuring Frankie tearing up when he learns that his pal Tyler has been arrested. In case you hadn't noticed, children's crying scenes were a popular staple in silent films, due in large part to Jackie Coogan's performance in *The Kid*. Even Frankie is brought into the action.

Astride a pony, Frankie rides full bore after a bad guy and eventually lassoes him! Frankie was ten years old at the time. Tyler cuts an imposing figure next to diminutive Frankie. The massive Tyler grabs Frankie at one point, and his hand is almost as wide as Frankie's waist. Nicely photographed in what appear to be the hills around Simi Valley, California, it's a shame that only one in the series has survived. After the series concluded, Tyler would remain a cowboy star until the early years of talking pictures. In 1940 he appeared as the mummy in Universal's *The Mummy's Hand*, and in 1941 he appeared as the title character in Republic Pictures serial classic, *The Adventures of Captain Marvel*. After World War II, his career faltered. Suffering from rheumatoid arthritis, the destitute Tyler moved in with family members in Michigan where he died in his early 50's in 1954. Frankie would occasionally run into Tyler in later years and both remembered the series with fond memories.

The Tyler/Darro series was produced by Film Booking Office of America, better known simply as FBO. In the early 1920's the British-based production company was purchased by Joseph Kennedy, patriarch of the Kennedy family based in Boston. Once in charge of the company, Kennedy had no desire to produce well reviewed quality entertainment. He apparently used his film company as a magnet to attract young starlets and to make a quick buck or two in the process. He kept the budgets lean, under the $30,000 range. His films did well in undemanding locations, rural markets mostly. Films were just a small foot note in Kennedy's burgeoning financial empire, but for a period of five years, Frankie's boss was none other than the father or our 31st President, an irony well remembered by Frankie during his later years.

At the age of eight in 1926, Frankie appeared in an amazing eighteen films. At an age when most kids would nowadays be in school and then out playing with friends, Frank Sr. made sure his son was on the set, ready to work and was bringing in the cash. Among the releases that year were long forgotten titles such as *Hearts and Spangles*, released by Lumas Picture Corporation. The film's story revolved around a young man who joins a circus and falls in love with the bareback rider. *Variety* stated in its review that "Frankie Darro turned in nice work as the kid." Frankie left the cinema circus for the carnival in *The Carnival Girl* a five reel film starring Marion Mack.

Frankie plays Mack's brother, who performs as an ape in the carnival. After the death of their mother, they are left in the guardianship of Sigmund the strongman, who coincidentally is also a rum runner. Next, Frankie was back at Metro-Goldwyn for *Mike*, starring Sally O'Neil and William Haines. The story revolved around a widowed father, a brakeman for the railroad and his four children, with Frankie playing the youngest of his children. The film was shot mostly at the El Cajon Pass near San Diego. While filming, the cast slept in Pullman cars at night and filmed at various railroad sites during the day. Playing Frankie's older brother was Frank "Junior" Coghlan, an up and coming child star himself. Coghlan was paid $75/week for his participation in the film. Frankie, the veteran of the children, would have been paid at least a little more than that. Frankie and "Junior" Coghlan's paths would cross again with the advent of talking pictures. Also in the cast was the black actor Fred Toones who went by the nickname "Snowflake". He too would work with Frankie a decade later.

The only film of Frankie's to survive from 1926 is *Kiki*, based on a play by Picard and Bellusso, who were paid a whopping $75,000 for the film rights. The film was directed by the noted Clarence Brown. Unfortunately the film has not aged well. Star Norma Talmadge comes across as a crazed stalker instead of the lovelorn gamin she is supposed to be playing. The main setting for the film is co-star Ronald Coleman's lavish home, where it quickly becomes stage bound for the remainder of the film's running time. Frankie plays Pierre, a young friend of Kiki's, at the start of the film, Frankie is seen selling newspapers and picking his nose, but then he disappears as the film moves indoors. Footage appears to be missing from the surviving print, so perhaps Frankie may have had a more substantial role in a longer version.

The year 1927 was almost as busy as the previous year for young Frankie. He appeared in a total of eight films. Three were in the Tyler series, *Cyclone of the Range, Tom's Gang, and Flying U Ranch* which was released on November 2. *Flying U Ranch* was photographed by Joseph Walker, who a few years later became Frank Capra's cinematographer of choice during Capra's heyday at Columbia. *Variety* noted the fine cinematography in its review of the picture, also noting that the Tyler/Darro films were doing well, but they also mentioned these as "aged stories."

It would be another eight years before Capra hit the big time with the release of *It Happened One Night*. In 1926 he was learning his comedic craft with Harry Langdon at First National Pictures. His second picture with the fast rising star was *Long Pants*. Frankie was hired to play Harry Langdon's character as a young boy. The scenes were filmed, but eventually cut, from the final release print. The production was a troubled one, with Langdon exerting his influence over Capra, and forcing Capra to eventually quit. The film was cut extensively prior to its release, leaving all of Frankie's footage on the cutting room floor. As released, it's a rather odd film, with a supposed comic highlight showing Langdon out in the woods trying to shoot his wife on their wedding day. It's been reported that a photo of Frankie appears in the film, but we'll have to wait and see if a longer version of the film is unearthed to view Frankie's few scenes. Frankie does receive credit for the film in various reference works, but he is not billed on the film itself.

Frankie's work at FBO was not limited to the Tyler westerns. FBO released *Her Father Said No*, a love story between a boxer and a woman who knows nothing of his chosen profession. To add to the drama, her wealthy father hates fighters. In its review, *Variety* stated, "Little Frankie Darro as an orphan that becomes the training camp mascot certainly lends himself for the sob stuff element." On August 5, FBO released *Judgment of the Hills*, the story of an illiterate brute living in the hills of Kentucky with his kid brother. The movie was based on a story that appeared in *Cosmopolitan* and starred Virginia Valli. *Variety* liked the film but not the title for some reason, and they gave Frankie another nice mention, "Darro, juvenile known mostly for his work in 'quickie' westerns with Tom Tyler, here is head and shoulders above any of his previous stuff." Frankie received above the title first billing for the first time, in the newspaper ads. Unfortunately the film is considered lost.

Frankie wound up in a twenty second bit in the MGM Clarence Brown production of *Flesh and the Devil*. Dressed in a military uniform, Frankie asks Fraulein Hurffe for a dance. She rebuffs his advances and Frankie moves on with the same request to his costar Lars Hanson's sister. She accepts his invitation, and his quick bit in the film is over.

John Gilbert and Greta Garbo starred in the film, which holds up remarkably well today. Also in 1927 Frankie appeared in *Moulders of Men*, directed by Ralph Ince, the man who gave Frankie his start in motion pictures.

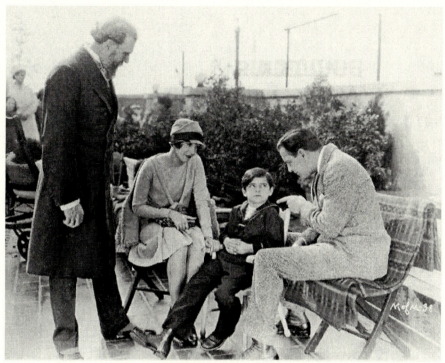

*Moulders of Men-*1927.

FBO gave Frankie star billing in *Little Mickey Grogan.* The story revolves around an architect who is slowly loosing his sight. Frankie plays the title character. A review noted FBO was trying to make Frankie a star with the film but that the script left him down. The film was released on February 29, 1928. FBO released another eight westerns in the Tyler/Darro series the same year.

The series continued its popularity with titles such as *Tyrant of Red Gulch* and *Terror Mountain,* which *Variety* called "first rate." Another in the series, *Phantom of the Range,* has Tyler portraying an actor stranded in a small town where he must revert to his original occupation of a cowpuncher. The film was originally reviewed by *Variety* running a scant forty-five minutes, it dismissed the film. Three months later on May 2, 1928, the film was back in a sixty minute version. This time *Variety* actually liked the film, making note that it had plenty of action. *Variety* wasn't so kind with the November

14 release of *Avenging Rider*, noting that "thing is generally nonsensical and abnormally hacked."

On November 12, 1928 it was announced to the press that the ongoing fight over Frankie and his money was finally settled. Ada in addition to the money was also looking for custody of her son. Frankie was nine years old and earning $300.00 a week, when the judge announced that Frankie was to, "be given the chance in life to which he is entitled and which has been denied him thus far." The judge's ruling was to give custody of Frankie to a third party, the identity of which was to be named at a later date. For some reason it looks like this never happened, for Ada would spend the rest of her life fighting for Frankie's earnings.

Frankie and the Singer Midgets on the set of *The Circus Kid*-1928.

On December 19 FBO released one of its bigger budget films entitled *The Circus Kid.* The film could have been the story of

Frankie's young life. The two leads were Helene Costello and Joe E. Brown. Frankie's role is rather small, but in the scenes he does have, he is utterly charming. Frankie gets to perform a few cartwheels early in the film when he is supposed to be standing in formation at an orphanage where he lives. The cartwheels create havoc when he crashes into the headmaster, played by Lionel Belmore. Unfortunately, once he's adopted by the circus, he does not get to perform any other acrobatics in the movie. After filming was completed, the revolution of talking pictures was starting to sweep the nation. Rural theatres were able to resist conversion to sound for a while, but larger theaters in the big cities had to pony up the cash and install sound equipment. Silent films quickly became relics of a bygone era.

Frankie, Patricia Caron and Tom Tyler in *Idaho Red*-1929.

Realizing that *The Circus Kid* could make more money as a sound film, FBO shot a sound comedy prologue for the film which featured

George LeMarie. *Variety* called the film's story "old" and "trite", but liked the prologue inadvertently commenting on the death of silent films.

The final four Tyler/Darro films were released in 1929. By now, the long-running series had just about run its course. *Trail of the Horse Thieves* was released on February 13. *Variety* made note that "Tyler overacts to a painful degree, and little Frankie seems to be aping him." March 29 saw the release of *Gun Law* the story and scenario were written by prolific western writer Oliver Drake. Still, *Variety* panned it, calling the film "a typical western…cheaply made, badly constructed." The series concluded with the release of *Idaho Red* and *Pride of the Pawnee.*

Realizing that the revolution in talking pictures was not just a fad, Joseph Kennedy announced in January 1928 that RCA had acquired a "substantial interest" in FBO. Since RCA had developed its own motion picture sound recording device, called Photophone, FBO would be able to enter the age of talking pictures without a huge capital outlay. The sound revolution would be the death knell for a myriad of low budget companies that couldn't afford to convert to sound.

Later that same year, Kennedy and RCA President David Sarnoff signed a deal with the Keith-Albee-Orpheum organization to acquire their string of vaudeville houses. This acquisition would give FBO an outlet for its talking pictures. It would no longer be forced to show its films in rural areas, far from big cities, where the screens were held in monopoly by the major studios. The merger created a $300 million corporation that was renamed RKO. Just when it looked like Kennedy could become a real Hollywood player, he resigned. With the demise of FBO Frankie was without a studio contract.

As the sound revolution swept through Hollywood, many of the popular stars of the silent era fell out of favor with the general public. While some lost favor due to their voices, which didn't always match their looks, others like John Gilbert couldn't adapt to the techniques of acting in sound films, and some like Douglas Fairbanks were aging and quickly considered relics of the past as new younger actors, mostly stage trained, came on the scene.

For most child actors, once they would hit their early adolescence, they would see their careers grind to a halt. They became has-beens before most kids would begin their first jobs. Frankie, however, had an ace in the hole-his voice. As he entered early adolescence, he developed a distinctive, light, raspy vocal intonation that was tailor made for sound pictures. His rough voice was due in some part to his smoking habit. He became a heavy smoker by the age of fifteen. Frankie had another plus in that his exuberant acting style also fit perfectly with early sound films. The difficult part was finding a studio that wanted his services.

Frank Sr. tried to interest some of the majors in hiring his talented twelve year old son, but without luck. Since Frankie had spent most of his career in B films, he was almost an unknown to the major studios, so Frank Sr. began knocking on the doors of the studios that lined "poverty row", the section of Hollywood that housed the independent and B film production companies. He hit pay dirt on Sunset Drive. A newly formed company with the imposing name of Sono Art-World Wide Pictures was working out of a small studio with the equally imposing name of Ralph M. Like's International Film Studio. Sono was about to shoot its inaugural feature entitled *Rainbow Man*, and they hired Frankie as the costar. The comedy starred Eddie Dowling and Marion Nixon, with Frankie receiving third billing. The story was a popular one in the early days of sound films. A man who has a minstrel act falls in love with a woman whose family detests people in show business. The film was released on April 24, 1929. *Variety* commented favorably on Frankie, noting that "Darro… [was a] sufficiently clever performer to make all comedy points register." *Rainbow Man* was followed by another Sono Art-World Wide Film. *Blaze 'O Glory*. In this film an entertainer is put on trial for murder. The man he murdered was thought by him to be his wife's lover. Musical numbers were inserted throughout the film, which was called "strange" in a trade review of the time. Eddie Dowling was again the star, and Frankie once again received third billing. The film is considered lost, but fortunately the soundtrack has survived.

Realizing that Sono Art-World Wide Pictures was pretty much bottom of the barrel, Frank Sr. went back to knocking on doors. He knew he had a talented son and was determined to keep him working. Two more doors would soon open, one at Mascot, the up and coming B studio, and the other over at Warner Bros.

CHAPTER 4
MASCOT

As America entered the fresh new decade of the 1930's, life couldn't get much worse for most Americans. Late in 1929 the stock market crashed, sending the country spiraling into a depression that would take a world war to end it. Three quarters of the country was unemployed, and what little money people had went for basic food. If any cash was left in the budget, it might be spent on a little entertainment-and that meant movies for most folks.

On December 17, 1930 Frankie turned thirteen years old. As mentioned earlier, most former child actors would be hard pressed to find bit parts as they matured into their teens, but Frankie had an advantage over most. The advantage, later to be his second biggest disadvantage, would be his size. Frankie was only 5'3" as he entered his teen years. The growth spurt that most young boys go through in their early teens just never materialized for him. The advantage of being of short stature enabled him to play young teen roles well into his twenties. At this point in his career, little thought was given to longevity in the business or even of film quality for that matter. Frank Sr. would seek employment for his talented son wherever and whenever he could. Frank Sr. had also given little thought to Frankie's education. There were teachers on the set assigned to children, but the job of acting always was the priority of the day. If Frankie was needed for a scene and he was in the middle of a lesson, he was simply yanked out and put in front of the camera. Frankie also had a knack for simply disappearing between takes. Going on an impromptu horseback ride or climbing a tree was a lot more fun than having a teacher trying to explain the multiplication tables to you.

The men who formed the early film industry in Hollywood, more often than not, are portrayed as pioneers. But gamblers would also be an apt description, especially in the case of one Nathaniel "Nat" Levine. Levine was born in New York City on July 26, 1899. Like so many others in film production, he started out in the exhibition side, working for the Marcus Lowe Theater chain. After a nearly ten year apprenticeship, Levine knew where the real money was to be made and tried his hand at producing. He was able to raise $10,000 to buy the distribution rights to a completed but as yet unreleased film entitled *Every Women's Problem*. He released the film in 1921. When the film grossed almost four times his initial investment, Levine realized his gamble had paid off, and he also realized where the big money in the film business was to be found.

By the mid 1920's, Levine had set up offices at the Metropolitan Studios on Las Palmas in the heart of Hollywood. He kept busy cranking out countless serials and B action films. As with so many other independent studios at the time, with long forgotten names such as Tiffany, Chesterfield-Invincible, or Sono Art-World Wide Pictures, the method of production was to make a film so cheaply that with the costs low, it was bound to make a profit. The independents knew that they couldn't compete with the major studios, even if they had the bigger budgets. The majors had the stars in iron-clad, multiyear contracts. Besides, the major studios owned all the large glamorous movie palaces that would only show the films produced by the studios that owned them.

For stars, the independents usually relied on actors on their way down the Hollywood success ladder, or if they were lucky, on their way up. In a few cases this could be most fortunate. Levine cast a young John Wayne in three of his serials. When Wayne hit the big time with the release of *Stagecoach* in 1939, the three serials would prove to be an enduring commodity, even years later into the age of home video.

Since action movies were Levine's staple, it was only a matter of time until he would cross paths with Frankie.

At the age of fourteen Frankie, or more accurately, Frank Sr., signed a non-exclusive contract with Nat Levine's Mascot Pictures.

A veteran at such a young age, Frankie knew what was expected of him. In an interview a couple of years after signing on with Mascot, he summed up his appeal. "I don't know a thing about art, and I seldom do any serious reading. I suppose it would help me, but I'm not making out so bad. I don't think my fans would like me to go highbrow anyway. I read every [fan] letter I get and I have a pretty good idea of what people expect of me. If I can satisfy them, that's all that's necessary."

First up at Mascot for Frankie would be *The Vanishing Legion*, a twelve chapter serial. Even diehard serials buffs would be hard pressed to defend most of the serials produced by Mascot. The serial had yet to enter its golden age. That was still a few years in the future, when Levine would merge his studio with Republic Studios and Universal would release its classic *Flash Gordon*. By the early 1940's, Republic had turned the serial genre into an art form, but at Mascot it was destined to remain a commodity.

Serials would generally run twelve or fifteen chapters, with the first chapter running slightly longer-20 to 30 minutes, than the follow up chapters. The theaters would show one chapter per week, with each ending showing a cliffhanging moment, such as a woman tied on the railroad tracks with a locomotive bearing down on her. The hope was that the audience would find this so suspenseful that they would have to return the following week to view the resolution.

The Vanishing Legion began production in May 1931. It was scheduled for a twenty-one day shoot. However, Director B. Reeves Eason, nicknamed Breezy for his quick-shooting methods, wrapped up production in only eighteen days. The story concerns Cardigan, (portrayed by western film stalwart Harry Carey), who is planning to drill land for oil. His efforts are being thwarted by a villain known as "The Voice", who communicates to his henchman via short wave radio. A group of mysterious horsemen, known as The Vanishing Legion, at first hinder but then eventually help, Carey in his effort. The Vanishing Legion is a sort of precursor to the "Thunder Riders", who would be led by Frankie in his final serial for Mascot, *The Phantom Empire*.

In the story Carey is aided by his young friend, Jimmie Williams, (played by Frankie). Since Frankie's father has been accused of murder and is on the run, Carey becomes the father figure to young Frankie. To delve into the plot more deeply would be futile and ultimately meaningless. Frankie isn't given many heavy dramatic scenes this time, but the few he does have are quite well handled. In chapter one Frankie believes his father has been killed by Rex, a wild horse. Frankie holds his dad in his arms. Fred Hearn, who plays his dad, wildly overacts, while Frankie projects a touching, controlled hysteria. Frankie is given many opportunities to ride a supposedly wild horse bareback. With typical Darro ease he does a wonderful flying rear mount onto Rex in chapter five. One can see the true joy in Frankie's face as he rides bareback on Rex through the mountains of Kernville. It must have been like a dream come true for young Frankie. The horse is played by Rex the Wonder Horse, who had a reputation of being a bit cantankerous, but the horse shows only love and respect in his scenes with Frankie. Rex would return with Frankie in *The Devil Horse*, playing the title character.

The adult stars include Carey and Edwina Booth, both recent stars of the popular MGM movie *Trader Horn.* Carey, as always, projects a strong leadership quality. Unfortunately, Booth is perhaps the most inept leading lady in serial history. Frankie's natural style of acting is in stark contrast to the others in the cast, with the exception of Carey. Most of the other cast members seem to be trying to out "act" one another. Boris Karloff supplies the voice to the villain in all but one chapter. Karloff was still a few months away from making cinema history in *Frankenstein* and received no billing for his effort.

Frankie was billed fifth in the cast and was paid a flat $1000 for his work on the serial. During this time actors were paid a flat fee for their work. Residuals were still two decades into the future. One of Frankie's costars was famed stuntman, Yakima Canutt (who would direct Frankie in *The Lawless Rider* in 1954). The film was shot at the Prudential lot near Kernville, California and at Universal Studios. The serial is pretty challenging to view today, even for diehard serial buffs. A DVD release caused a minor furor with film buffs when a scene showed Fred Hearns (who plays Frankie's father) kissing Frankie on the mouth in a rather lingering fashion. The scene was cut short by the DVD's producer, citing disrespect for Frankie. Strangely, the excised scene is used as an extra on the disc.

A few months later, in November that same year, Levine started production on Frankie's next serial entitled *The Lightning Warrior.* It was another brisk shoot, wrapped up in just twenty-three days. The

Lightning Warrior of the title was none other than Rin Tin Tin, famous German Shepherd star, making what would turn out to be his final film appearance. According to the film's story, Rin Tin Tin was named The Lightning Warrior due to his fighting prowess. For his efforts Rin Tin Tin (or more appropriately his owner) was paid a hefty $5000, a nice sum in the middle of the Great Depression when the average human worker was making less than $3,000 per year! Frankie was paid $2000 this time, but since he was still four years away from his eighteenth birthday, his salary went to Frank Sr. Frankie and his canine costar couldn't even benefit monetarily from all their hard work! At least the two adult leads, future Warner Brothers star George Brent and *Gold Rush* costar Georgina Hale, could deposit their own salary checks in the bank, if they could find one open, of course.

The plot is convoluted, even by Mascot standards. It seems that settlers are being chased off their land by a group of Indians. The Indians are being controlled by a mysterious figure known as the Wolfman, who is not a lycanthrope by the way. When Frankie's father is killed by the Indians, Frankie becomes the sole owner of the valuable mine. Alan Scott (played by George Brent) tries to find out the true identity of the Wolfman with help from Diane (played by Georgina Hale), Frankie and of course Rin Tin Tin. At the conclusion we find out that a man named McDonald (played by Frank Brownlee) was actually the Wolfman and that the Indians were in fact a group of white men dressed up as Indians.

The setting of the serial was the town of Sainte Suzanne, in reality the often used Prudential lot in Kernville California, located about 120 miles north east of Hollywood. The interiors were shot at the Tec-Art Studios in North Hollywood and at Universal Studios. In chapter four we see the Wolfman's hideout for the first time and it's the ubiquitous Bronson caves, perhaps the most often used natural film location of all time.

In chapter nine Rin Tin Tin saves Frankie from drowning, but ultimately the canine star doesn't have much to do. He was getting a little long in the tooth by this stage of his career and was used mostly for running here and there around the beautiful Kern River locations. For the strenuous scenes, they used a stunt double. In chapter eleven,

Rinty shows he still has some spark left. When George Brent is locked in a jail cell, the canine star saunters over to the cell door, removes the key from the door with his mouth, and hands the key to Brent! He also gets to shove three of the bad guys off a cliff and then steals their guns!

As Frankie would demonstrate with horses many times over, he shows a real affinity for Rinty. It's a shame they weren't given much to do together. The actions scenes in the serial are speeded up to give an exciting look, but all it does in reality is give the serial a dated jerky look. The plot calls for the good guys to constantly try and guess the identity of the Wolfman, so we are subjected to countless lines like, "It's Indian George he must be the Wolfman!"

With its ultra confusing story line (just try and follow the chapter recaps, especially toward the end) and the non-existent musical score, it is a very difficult serial to watch. It served its purpose at the time, but it's of little interest today unless you're a serial completist.

By 1932 Nat Levine had serial production down to a science. By keeping the budgets low, in the $60,000 range, he was able to gross $600,000 by the time the serial was played out. It's even more amazing when you realize that the individual episodes rented for only $5.00 a piece.

As mentioned earlier, Frankie had the ability to disappear when it was time for his on-set tutoring. He could also make himself scarce at home. One of his favorite pastimes was going to the beach. He loved the ocean, and it made for a great getaway from the confines of Hollywood life. One day Frankie and a friend hitchhiked to the beach, something they did on a regular basis. After spending the day swimming in the Pacific Ocean, they hitchhiked back. The driver who offered them a ride was none other than Ben Turpin, the famous cross-eyed comedian. Apparently his crossed eyes affected his driving ability because he was such a terrible driver that he scared the hell out of Frankie and his friend. They both vowed never to hitchhike again.

With his son under contract to Mascot and also bouncing back between Warner Bros. assignments, Frankie was a busy kid indeed. This would have made any father happy, but Frank Sr. found even more jobs for Frankie, who was now more and more in demand.

Frank Sr. had no idea how much longer his son's popularity would last, so he kept Frankie working as much as possible. He snagged his son a small but important role in the 1931 MGM release *The Sin of Madelon Claudet*. Helen Hayes won her first Academy Award for her performance as the title character. Her sin in the movie was that of bearing an illegitimate child. The child (named Lawrence Claudette) is portrayed by Frankie in an uncredited performance. Frankie's character, as an adult is portrayed by Robert Young.

The pre-code film has Hayes turning to prostitution and thievery in order to pay for her son's medical school education; all the while, the adult Lawrence believes his mother to be dead. It was a small role for Frankie, but a job at MGM would be very impressive on his resume.

Frankie's mother Ada, who had not been in good health for years, died in 1932, finally ending a long struggle to benefit from Frankie's income. As mentioned earlier, the court had planned to settle the matter but unfortunately it did not. This left Frank Sr. exclusively in charge of Frankie's income. Frank Sr.'s idea to watch over the money was to simply spend as much as he could as quickly as possible.

Away from Mascot, the following year Frankie appeared in *Amateur Daddy*, released by Fox on April 10, 1932. The film was based on the novel "Scotch Valley" written by Mildred Cram. Frankie plays Pete Smith, one of four children living on a rural farm. As the story opens, the children's mother has died and their father has apparently abandoned them years earlier. Enter Jim Gladden (played by Warner Baxter), who has witnessed the death of a man he believes is the brood's father. Gladden promises the dying man that he will look after his children. Trouble begins as soon as the stalwart Baxter arrives on the farm. Sally, the oldest but still underage-daughter, has a romantic interest in Baxter, but that's just about the least of his problems.

The neighbor's wife, Lotti Pelgram (played with relish by Rita La Roy) has desires for Baxter herself. Within seconds of their meeting she goes so far as to force a kiss on him and then starts to unbutton his shirt. Baxter can barely take a breath before beating a hasty retreat. As if there weren't enough problems, it turns out that Baxter was on the wrong farm all along! The children's real father finally shows up having just been released from prison, and with his attitude it's clear that he should still be incarcerated.

The myriad of problems are all worked out in the finish, the farm is saved and the bad guys are killed. Obviously a little plot heavy but with enough plot twists and turns and a pre-code raciness, the film still holds interest today. Frankie is billed eight. He has a special affinity with the family mule Queenie. The usually stubborn mule smiles on command and follows Frankie's orders implicitly, all the while ignoring the other kids. Frankie is at odds with the Pelgran son, Sam Jr. (played by Joe Hackey), and a rough and tumble fight ensues, with Frankie the victor. While he has limited screen time, Frankie plays the role confidently and with his special brand of pathos, never going over the top, as was the custom so much of the time in the early days of sound films.

Frankie's home studio during the silent days, FBO had seen a massive transformation in the intervening years and it emerged as one of the major studios in the early sound years, after being renamed RKO. Frankie returned to the studio in 1932 for *Way Back Home*. It was another story of rural America in the 1930's based on the popular radio serial character Seth Parker (played by Robert Lord). Parker is a preacher in Maine who has taken care of an orphan boy named Robbie Turner (played by Frankie). To say the least it's disconcerting when we see Frankie playing a rural lad dressed in short pants and a straw hat. There is a tender scene between Robbie and Parker when Robbie finds out the truth that Parker is not his real father. Robbie cries and the scene is not only effective for Frankie but extremely touching as well. The film turns terrifyingly realistic when Robbie's real father breaks into the house to kidnap him. It all turns out well for Robbie, and what at first seems like bizarre casting, actually turns out to be another top notch performance for young Frankie. Unfortunately, the film as a whole is pretty much of a dud. It starts out as a rural comedy and then turns so drama. Ultimately it succeeds as neither. A young Bette Davis plays the lovestruck Mary Lucy, but you would be hard pressed to find even a hint of her talented performances to come.

For Frankie it was back to Mascot. The budgets were smaller, but the billing was better, and they had come to realize that Frankie could carry a film, if only a lowly twelve chapter serial. Levine released four serials in 1932, with the one starring Frankie entitled *The Devil Horse*. The pressbook refers to Levine as "The Serial King" and refers to Frankie as "the screen's most popular child star." The story of *The Devil Horse* was based on a 1926 feature of the same name produced by Hal Roach. The original featured ace stuntman Yakima Canutt, who also appears in this serial as well. Footage from the original also shows up in this version.

The story this time around has Frankie's character, (portrayed as a young child by child actor Carl Russell) watching while his father is killed by horse thieves. All alone in the world, Frankie grows up as a feral boy in the mountains, where he is befriended by a famous missing racehorse named El Diablo. Frankie, who has lost the ability to talk, communicates with the horse by the use of a whinny. Harry Carey plays an undercover marshall who is looking for the murderer of his younger bother. He is joined on his quest by Frankie and The Devil Horse.

The serial obviously had a larger budget than the previous entries, but Levine ran into production delays during location filming in Arizona. Levine had originally slated Rex the Wonder Horse to star in the serial but balked at his handler's high asking price. He had already committed ten grand to Carey, and three grand for Frankie. Instead of Rex, Levine used a three year old stallion. The horse looked fine, but due to his inexperience in front of the camera the animal slowed down production. In an effort to save money due to the cost over runs, Levine came up with a novel idea. He would use recap or cheat episodes. Cheat episodes were chapters in which characters would recall events that had happened in previous episodes. Footage from those episodes then would be used to fill time in the new chapter. This money saving-device would be in regular use in the later Republic serials.

Flashbacks occurred in chapters 5, 8, 9, 11 and 12 of *The Devil Horse*. The device certainly saved on production expenses, but slowed down the flow of the story. As mentioned earlier, Frankie does not speak in the early chapters but uses a type of whinny. It is not until chapter eight that Frankie is able to put enough words together to form a coherent sentence. The serial showcases, once again, Frankie's wonderful agility on horse-back. The serial is given a musical score this time, albeit an incongruous classical one, but nevertheless there is music, which certainly helps move the action along. The story ends on a rather depressing note. Frankie must give up the Devil Horse to its rightful owner. Frankie walks toward his four hoofed friend, and the horse meets Frankie half way. Then Frankie puts his arms around the neck of the horse and starts to cry, and the film ends, not the usually happy ending for a serial but simply another testimony to young Frankie's acting ability. He is able to convey such emotion, without even uttering a word.

The Mascot serial *The Wolf Dog*-1933.

Next was the 1933 release of *The Wolf Dog.* The serial features the same type of title card opening that was used for *The Devil Horse* only in this case it is, "a story of a man, a dog, and a boy." The man is played by George J. Lewis, perennial serial and B western actor, and the dog is none other than Rin Tin Tin, Jr., son of the original Rinty. In the story Lewis, a radio operator on a steamship has invented a so-called "Lightning Ray." As he states early on, "As long as airplanes, battleships, and submarines use oil and gasoline my Lightning Ray will blow them to pieces." People with inventions like the Lightning Ray are usually the villains in serials, but in this plot Lewis plans to hand over his device to the government. Frankie's character has been raised in the wilds by his stepmother, who eventually tells him that he is in reality the son of a wealthy shipping magnate. Leaving his mom to find his wealthy father, he meets up with a feral dog who will help him on his quest. Frankie befriends Lewis aboard a ship, and the trio wind up in Los Angeles. Brymer, the current head of the steamship line that was co-owned by Frankie's late father, wants Frankie killed so that he can have sole ownership of the company.

Once again, Levine employs flashbacks in order to save money. The device is used in chapters 4, 7, 8, 10 and 12. In another bid to save money, he extended the running time of the chapter recaps that would open each episode. Sixteen year old Frankie plays a thirteen year old, but due to his size and youthful appearance, this was really no stretch. Frankie was paid $4000 this time around and received third billing.

Perhaps due to his getting a bit older, Frankie is given more to do in this serial. He is given more dialogue and his character is more important to the story. The story itself is fast paced and less convoluted than the previous efforts. Interesting locations such as steamships, shipping docks, speedboats on the bay, and interesting wilderness areas-all help to make *The Wolf Dog* Frankie's best serial yet. Even Rin Tin Tin, Jr. acquits himself well. In one amazing scene we see him swimming in the middle of a bay just seconds after the speedboat he was on has exploded; in another he comes crashing through a plate glass window with the determination of a veteran. His role is actually more important to the serial than the one his famous father had in *The Lightning Warrior*. The ending of *The Wolf Dog* is a bit grisly. The villain, Bryan (played by Hale Hamilton), falls from a ship's block and tackle into the water, where he is shredded to death by the ship's propellers. Only his screams are heard as we watch

George J. Lewis's horrified face. But since he had been trying to kill off Frankie for twelve chapters, it was a fate well deserved. The ending aside, *The Wolf Dog* still holds up pretty well over seventy years after its initial release.

With plenty of money rolling in, Frank Sr. decided to take the matter of Frankie's education a little more seriously. He enrolled his talented son at the popular Lawlor's Professional School, located at Hollywood Boulevard near Western Avenue in Hollywood. Lawlor's alumni would eventually include such popular actors as Mickey Rooney, Betty Grable, Jane Withers and Judy Garland. One of Frankie's classmates was Peggy Montgomery, the former child star known as Baby Peggy. She developed a crush on Frankie, but she knew Frankie was running with a fast crowd and her mother watched her like a hawk. She did manage to at least stay friends with Frankie, even going so far as to interview him for a book she had planned to write about his life. The book idea never went further than a few interviews unfortunately. Viola F. Lawlor, the head of the school, knew of Frankie's childhood and felt sorry for his upbringing and as such, admitted to spoiling him.

Before Frankie's mom, Ada, died she had lived across the street from the famous school. The only way she could get an occasional look at her son was through the window of her apartment when Frankie arrived and then left for the day. By the time of his enrollment however, education was of little importance for Frankie. When he applied himself he could learn just about anything, but his life revolved around his acting and his early discovery of girls, so the lessons at school were of little importance to him. He was respected enough by the other students to be eventually elected the head of the drama club.

Besides being a prodigious producer of serials, Levine turned out sixteen features as well. In May 1933, Frankie began work on the first of two features for Mascot. *Laughing at Life* was the story of a carefree gunrunner, who starts revolutions for a lark; A sort of an early version of the Marlon Brando movie *Burn*, but without the social conscience. Victor McLaughlin plays the gunrunner. Without a strong willed-director to keep him halfway sedated as John Ford did in

The Informer, McLaughlin would mug his way through a performance. Here, he comes across as arrogant and perhaps a bit crazy. The director was Ford Beebe, an "old school" type of director, who was still wearing jodhpurs while directing Bomba the Jungle Boy films in the mid 50's. While certainly a competent director of action films, Beebe was not one to bring out the subtle nuisances of someone's performance.

Levine used almost his entire serial stock company in supporting roles and bit parts. Noah Beery, Guinn "Big Boy" Williams and even Henry B. Walthall show up for a few brief scenes and then are gone. Frankie is billed an astonishing seventeenth in the opening credits. He pops up early on, playing a South American revolutionary with the name of Chonga, in the fictitious country of Alturous. Frankie attempts a Hispanic accent in some of his scenes, but drops it all together in others. At one point in the film Frankie is caught stealing some apples, in order to escape he shouts, "Viva la revolucion!" and starts a march of dissidents unhappy with El Presidente (played by D.W. Griffith regular Henry B. Wathall). Frankie pops up occasionally throughout the film and he even helps McLaughlin escape his doom at the conclusion of the film by bringing him a horse with which to escape. The seventy-one minute film is not really bad but rather, sadly dull and plodding. Frankie doesn't add much to the film, and with his flimsy accent possibly detracts from it. Levine actually had this film reviewed by *The New York Times*. Unfortunately, it read in part, "The producers seemed to have pounced upon most of Hollywood's freelance actors, giving them parts usually meted out of extras. But it's all a waste of talent and possibly, plot."

Early in 1934 Frankie returned for what would be his penultimate serial for Levine, the twelve chapter *Burn 'Em Up Barnes*. Although the title was taken from a 1921 feature, the story was entirely new. This time, the story concerns Marjorie, (played by Lola Lane), owner of an auto repair shop. Unbeknownst to her, there is a valuable oil reserve under her property. An evil car racing magnate, (played by Jason Robards, Sr.) is trying to foreclose on her property so that he can grab all the oil for himself. Helping Marjorie fend off the gang is race car driver Barnes and, of course, Frankie. Frankie's father has been killed in the first chapter, so Barnes takes him under his wing.

The Mascot serial *Burn 'Em Up Barnes* with Lola Lane-1934.

Frankie's salary was upped to a whopping $5000 this time, and he certainly earned it. The serial is full of car chases, motorcycle chases, foot chases, gun fights and fist fights. Amazingly, it took a staff of four writers to concoct this story. Levine realized Frankie's importance to the success of his serials and gave him second billing in the credits and first billing in the print advertising. He's easily the best actor in the cast, full of youthful enthusiasm and athletic ability. Frankie is front and center all the way. Unfortunately, the same cannot be said of costar Jack Mulhall. Mulhall never seems to stop smiling. At one point in the serial he and Frankie are involved in a fight scene. Frankie acquits himself admirably, but Mulhall looks like he is scared of being punched out. At least it's one scene in which he's not smiling. About mid way through, the serial takes a turn to the surreal. The plot is all but forgotten when Mulhall gets a job as a movie stuntman. When the bad guys realize his new profession, it gives them a few new ways to try and bump him off. Mulhall does survive, of course, along with Marjorie and Frankie. The villains are caught with the use of a dictaphone. Ignoring the so-called comic relief from Tony, a supposed Italian working for Marjorie, the serial does its job well. There is plenty of location work in the San Fernando Valley and Hollywood. In chapter three we get a glimpse of Consolidated Film Industries, a company run by Herbert J. Yates, which would eventually merge with Mascot to form Republic Pictures. The serial might appeal more to old car buffs than to film fans. There are plenty of scenes featuring antiquated racecars, and old racetracks long forgotten except by diehard race fans. Frankie would go on to much better roles, of course, but Jack Mulhall's career was winding down, at least as a star. The onetime leading man of silent pictures would before long be reduced to doing bit parts. Late in his life, Frankie would run into Mulhall now and again, and the two would trade stories of the good old days, have lunch and promise to stay in touch. Mulhall who was twenty-nine years older than Frankie, outlived Frankie by three years.

Frankie and Gustav von Seyffetiz in *Little Men*-1934.

Levine turned to the sequel of a popular novel for Frankie's second and final feature for Mascot. "Little Women" by Louise May Alcott had been turned into a successful feature by RKO in 1933 starring Katharine Hepburn as Jo. Levine secured the rights to the novel's sequel entitled *Little Men*. It was a rather ambitious undertaking for the budget-conscious producer, who was known only as someone able to quickly crank out action films.

While nowhere near the production level of the RKO film, Levine didn't skimp on costs, and the film certainly looks polished. Frankie is billed second and plays Don, a streetwise orphan who moves into an orphanage run by Jo (played this time by Erin O'Brien-Moore). Once settled in the idyllic home for wayward boys, Frankie teaches them the joy of smoking a pipe, fist fighting, and other adolescent rights of passage. When asked to read what's written on the blackboard, Frankie admits, "I can't read very well," prompting laughter from the other boys. Frankie snaps back, "but I can lick any fella here…nobody's going to laugh at me!" Frankie is even given a chance to show off his athletic ability. At one point in the film, the kids put on a circus show, and Frankie entertains with some forward and back flips. The entertainment ends when Frankie slugs it out with one of the other boys, however. Levine even received press coverage for this production. A writer for *Picture Play* magazine was assigned to write a story on the filming. She quotes Frankie as telling fellow actor Junior Durkin between scenes, "Hey Junior, remember we gotta fight this afternoon, and if you don't pull your punches, I'll naturally beat the stuffin' out of yuh!" There was no mention whether Frankie was kidding or not.

The film is perhaps a little heavy on the dramatics, but still is very effective. The story revolves around Frankie, and he turns in the best performance in the film. The film also features an original musical score, something of a rarity for a Mascot film.

Frankie's popularity as a young actor was on the rise by the time *Little Men* was released. Mascot tied into his growing fame with the formation of the Frankie Darro Picture Stamp Club. For 25 cents, a fan of Frankie's could join the club, and in return they would receive a paperbound photo album, sans photos. The album featured a publicity photo of Frankie from *Burn 'Em Up Barnes*. The introduction, supposedly by Frankie, states that he shot all the photos for the album. Of course, Frankie never really shot any of the photos; they were all well known studio publicity shots. The album featured captions such as the one for Laurel and Hardy that read "Two swell guys." Every time a member of the club attended a showing of a chapter to *Burn 'Em Up Barnes*, they would receive two photo stamps. The club was a good way for fans to collect pictures of their favorite actors, and as Frankie states in the introduction, "…you will be thrilled when you see the dandy pictures of Buck Jones, Joe E. Brown, Tarzan, Jimmie Durante (sic) and many more of my actor friends." Added as a P.S. was, "Be sure to attend your theater each week so you can get all the picture stamps to fill your album." Theater owners would hold free matinees on occasion for members of the club.

Frankie's academic career at Lawlor seemed to be floundering but, there was another reason for Frankie to keep attending classes however. This was due to a young girl by the name of Virginia Gumm, who had impressed Frankie from the start. Virginia was a few months older than Frankie, born July 4, 1917. Virginia was the middle sister of the Gumm Sisters singing trio, the other two being Mary Jane and of course the youngest, Judy, who would eventually change her last name to Garland and quickly rise to stardom at MGM.

Frankie had originally met Virginia five years before, during a joint venture appearance. Virginia's parents, Fred and Ethel, brought their family out to California in 1927 in hopes of finding work for their talented offsprings. Frankie was hesitant to admit to a serious relationship, knowing that his fans wouldn't care for him dating just yet. But Virginia, nicknamed Jimmie, was something special, and Frankie was quickly smitten by her charms.

Frankie had had plenty of girlfriends by the time he met Virginia, but he had been able to keep them out of the public eye. The trick now would be to keep Virginia from knowing about all the other girls. Staying faithful to Virginia never really entered Frankie's mind. Being a successful and well known actor there were just too many girls he could have. He had discovered a quick way to meet girls for sex with no strings attached. Frankie had a friend who lived near Hollywood High School. After school the students would walk past the house on their way home. Frankie's friend would be in the front yard pulling weeds, with Frankie in the house looking out the front window. When they would spot a couple of cute girls, his friend would ask them if they would like to meet a movie star and point to Frankie waving at the front window. More often than not, the ploy worked.

Frankie's final effort for Mascot would be his best-the psychotronic serial masterpiece *The Phantom Empire*. Hollywood legend has it that writer Wallace MacDonald conceived the idea for the twelve chapter serial while under nitrous oxide during a dental visit. Folklore or fact, it's impossible to determine, but after initial viewing you might lean toward fact. The serial does use ideas found in other Mascot serials, most notable, *The Vanishing Legion*, but all and all, it's probably the most original, wackiest serial ever produced. The story concerns popular singing cowboy Gene Autry (played of course by Autry), who performs his radio show from his Radio Ranch resort. Helping him on the ranch are Frankie (playing a character named Frankie) and Betsy King Ross (playing Betsy). Frankie is the leader of a group of teens who ride horses while wearing capes and buckets on their heads, and call themselves The Junior Thunderiders. Meanwhile, a group of investors is trying to chase Autry off his ranch due to rich uranium deposits that which, unknown to Autry, lie beneath his property. As if this weren't enough, the ancient city of Murienia is located twenty miles below Radio Ranch and the ruler of Murienia is the evil Queen Tika, who has issued a death warrant for Autry.

Of the three leads, Frankie at age eighteen was the sole veteran. Autry had made only one earlier appearance in a film, a small role in a Ken Maynard western. In fact, Maynard was considered for the lead in *The Phantom Empire*. Levine even went so far as to print up publicity material with his name on it. Before filming began however, he was replaced due to his reputation of being difficult to work with. Betsy Ross King was a well known rodeo performer making her screen debut; she would make only two other screen appearances.

Many years later Frankie would recall how the neophyte Autry would approach the veteran Frankie for advice on acting and for words of wisdom on how to overcome his nervousness. Frankie was honored that Autry would ask him for help and tried to help as much as he could. Unfortunately, from viewing Autry's performance it's evident that the advice from Frankie was either not heeded or simply did not work. In Autry's defense, given the ridiculous dialogue and the story, it's doubtful that even a seasoned leading man could have come across better than Autry did. It's also worth wondering what Ken Maynard would have done with the role.

Frankie was given the majority of the plot dialogue to deliver, and he delivers the ridiculous lines with conviction. At the close of chapter nine, Frankie and Betsy are "killed" by an overdose of radium. Fortunately, at the beginning of chapter ten they are brought back to life in the radium removal chamber-it's that kind of serial!

Budgeted at $70,000, *The Phantom Empire* became the third most successful serial in Mascot history. Frankie would laugh when the title was mentioned. He was happy for Autry, as it was the beginning of his phenomenal movie career, but he thought the whole thing was so silly that no one should bother watching it. Autry, it seems, always had a special place in his heart for this wacky serial. A poster from the initial release is hanging in his museum in Griffith Park in Los Angeles, and in the gift shop you can purchase a coffee mug imprinted with the poster from the Belgium release. One of Autry's last television appearances, a documentary on AMC, was filmed at the Bronson Caves, which were used in the serial as the surface entrance to the underground city of Muriana. They even managed to find one of the silly-looking robots from the serial to make a cameo appearance. These robots were originally conceived for the MGM musical *Dancing Lady*, but the sequence with the robots was ultimately cut from the finished film. Years later the robots would return to serial work in *Captain Video*. Like Autry, Levine would not forget *The Phantom Empire* either. Shortly after its release he merged his company with Herbert J. Yates' Consolidated Film Industries to form Republic Pictures, perhaps the best B movie studio of all. However, Levine would stay with the new company only a few months before breaking away to produce movies on his own but would never achieve success again as a producer.

In 1940, with Gene Autry the leading movie cowboy in the country, Levine would re-edit the serial and release it as a feature to squeeze a few more dollars out of the film. He would re-title the feature *The Men With Steel Faces*, and release it to an unsuspecting public. A gambler to the end, Levine had lost millions in the years after his departure with Republic. The movies paid off for him, but not the racehorses. Levine wound up a manager of a movie theater in Southern California before dying on August 6, 1989, at the age of 90.

With the demise of Mascot, Frankie was left without a home studio, but there was still plenty of work for the new popular young star of B films.

CHAPTER 5
WARNER BROS.

Film buffs have long argued over which studio produced the greatest films during the Golden Age of Hollywood. Some prefer the sophisticated look of the films from Paramount and others the glossy musicals from RKO, but most would agree it was MGM, with its roster of stars and lavish budgets, that made it the greatest of all studios. They are all wrong. It was Warner Bros. Warners started out in a rather small studio on Sunset Boulevard in Hollywood before moving over the hill to their sprawling complex in Burbank in 1929.

While most of the major studios would bid for novels or Broadway plays for inspirations for their films, Warner's would rip its inspirations from newspaper headlines. No easy escapist entertainment here! Even its musicals had an edge to them. Warner Bros. stock company was second to none: Cagney, Bogart, Davis, and Flynn. Not even MGM with its "More stars than there are in Heaven" slogan could possibly compete.

While never a contract player for Warner's, Frankie was hired for nine films between 1931 and 1935. The first two had Frankie playing the juvenile part that would later be played by the adult lead. There would also be a good dramatic lead (even if he was not billed as the lead) in *The Mayor of Hell* followed by the film he was most proud of, *Wild Boys of the Road*.

First up was *The Public Enemy*, directed by William A. Wellman, ace Warner director who was given the appropriate nickname of Wild Bill. The film made James Cagney a star, as well it should. Cagney (playing gangster Tom Powers) is insolent, arrogant and, in a way only Cagney could make a gangster, sympathetic. The film opens with an eight minute prologue set in the year 1909. We see Powers and his pal Matt Doyle as young boys. The prologue is meant to humanize the gangsters by showing them growing up in the slums and getting involved with the Fagin-like gangster, Putty Nose. Powers has a brute for a father, and when his father whips him with a belt, young Powers lets out a fart in defiance. In a clever touch, we see the kids delivering beer, which would be their undoing as adults. Frankie plays a young Matt (who as an adult would be played by Eddie Woods). Frankie's buddy from the film, *Mike*, (Frank Coughlin, Jr.), plays Powers as a young boy.

Frankie and his father were living at 5522 Sierra Vista Ave. a small apartment complex just a few short blocks from Paramount Studios when Frank Sr. signed a contract on January 13, 1931. The contract paid Frankie $300.00 for one weeks work on the film. Frank Coughlin, Jr. received $350.00 for his week of work.

Frank Coughlin, Jr. was happy to be working with his pal Frankie again, but he soon realized that Frankie, who was a year and a half older than himself, had matured beyond his year. While the film was still in the rehearsal stage of production Frankie invited Coughlin to the movies one night in Hollywood. Only too happy to accept, he met up with Frankie in the balcony section of the movie theater, only to be surprised to find Frankie sitting between two young girls. Frankie gladly gave up his prized seat for Frank. In a flash the two girls grabbed both of Frank's hands and shoved them under the tops of their dresses so that he now had a firm grasp of their breasts. This was a first for young Coughlin. Frankie, sensing Frank's nervous discomfort, could barely contain his laughter. When the girls went to work trying to unbuckle his belt, Coughlin put a stop to their fun. Frankie's laughing brought an usher, and the quartet was quiet for the rest of the evening. A few days later Coughlin stopped by Frankie's apartment unannounced, just to say hello. When Frankie answered the door he was stark naked, except for a pair of women's panties on his head, and a towel hanging from his erect penis. One of the girls from the movie theater was lying naked on the sofa. Frankie invited him in, but Coughlin beat a hasty retreat, so perhaps, Frankie was living a lifestyle that Coughlin wanted no part of.

Filming on the movie began on January 25, 1931 on location at The May Co. a popular downtown Los Angeles department store. The scene called for Frankie and Frank to run through the store causing havoc to the patrons and sliding down the up escalator. Filming wrapped for the two Franks five days later on the 29th with their final scene showing them carrying beer outside of Paddy Ryan's saloon.

With the prologue finished, Wellman began shooting the main story with Cagney and the rest of the adult cast members.

The Public Enemy was released on May 15, 1931, and became an immediate hit. The film made a star out of Cagney and increased Wellman's stature at the studio. The two Franks benefited little from their appearance in the prologue, but the prologue is an important addition to the film as a whole. The film packs a strong emotional punch today, over seventy years after its release. At the time, even Cagney was worried the film was too strong.

Before the release, he wrote a letter to his mother, explaining that the mother and son in the movie were in no way meant to resemble Jimmy and his mom. Even the trade paper *Reel Journal* sent out a word of warning to the movie theaters. In its review of May 1931, it suggested, "This picture requires lively short subjects to brighten up the program a bit, for there is no comedy relief, and it will cast a depressing mood over the audience unless entertaining short subjects are run in conjunction with the picture."

Between scenes schooling while shooting *The Public Enemy* with
Frank Coghlan, Jr. -1931.

Frankie's next role for Warner's would be a duplicate of the type of role he played in *The Public Enemy*. This time he would play young Fodor in the prologue of the film *The Mad Genius*. In the story a young Russian boy named Fodor is being chased by his brute of a father. The father is played by an unrecognizable Boris Karloff, still a few months away from his famous role in *Frankenstein*. Trying to escape the whippings of his father, young Fodor gracefully leaps over fences, not unlike a deer. To achieve this effect, a harness was attached to Frankie, with fine wires attached to a weighted boom just off camera. The device made Frankie almost weightless and was pure joy for Frankie. Young Fodor escapes his father by seeking refuge in the wagon of a pair of traveling puppeteers played by John Barrymore and Charles Butterworth. After witnessing the fabulous leaps, Barrymore has the idea of training the young Fodor to be a great ballet dancer, a dancer he could never become due to a leg injury. Other than a mournful scream, Frankie has no dialogue. After the prologue he is replaced by the adult Fodor (played by Donald Cook). Unlike *The Public Enemy*, Frankie receives billing this time, eighth to be precise.

Barrymore's stardom was on the wane at the time of production, but only a few short years earlier he had been one of the most celebrated of all stage actors. His fame was not lost on Frankie, as he had the famous profile autograph a beautiful 11x14 photograph of himself. It was a treasure that Frankie would keep the rest of his life.

The Mad Genius is full of pre-code delights, such as unmarried sexual encounters, drug addiction, and so forth. A few short years later in 1934, the strict censorship laden production code would be enforced changing the tone of American films for three decades. Anton Grot out did himself with the striking production design, including the pre-*Citizen Kane* use of ceilings. The only weak link in the film is Donald Cook as the adult Fodor. Cook is rather bland in the role, and his character is perhaps too free of bitterness after having been raised in such miserable circumstances. It should be noted that in its review for the film, *Variety* misspelled Frankie's last name as Darrow.

Frankie's next film for Warner's was released on Oct. 29, 1932. The film was entitled *Three On A Match* and he was in a brief scene in yet another prologue. The story revolves around three young women who as youngsters were best of friends. After going their separate ways, they reunite as adults. The film opens at the playground of their grade school. Frankie plays Bob, one of the school children. He is standing next to one of the girls, watching another girl use playground equipment, when she does some flips and in the process exposes her panties. The girl next to Frankie says to him, "Gee, I hate black bloomers, don't you?" Without batting an eye Frankie responds, "What color are yours?" The girl states, "Pink." Without saying a word, Frankie gives a sly smile. Later in the prologue we see Frankie at the graduation ceremony smoking a cigarette, with a couple other boys.

Unlike his two previous Warner Bros. films, his character is not carried over to the adult part of the story. The film is another pre-code delight. Featuring copious amounts of drinking, women in underwear, affairs, drugs, and suicide, it's a fast moving, excellent film that features early performances by Bette Davis and Humphrey Bogart. In 1938 Warner's remade the film as *Broadway Musketeers.*

Although Frankie had only brief appearances in his first three Warner Bros. films, it did give him an opportunity to act in A films at a major studio. As good as his work was at Mascot, the films and serials were considered little more than fillers at the time. But Warner Bros. was the "big time", and in his next film for the studio he was given a chance to shine in a leading role. Although he receives only sixth billing, Frankie is the true star of his next Warner film, *The Mayor of Hell.*

Unfortunately, for the brothers Warner, the Great Depression was now hitting the film industry, and hitting it hard. People were lining up at the box office for a little entertainment, but the studio was operating at a loss. At the end of 1933, the studio racked up a loss of $6,291,748. To ease the cash crunch all studio personnel took a 50% pay cut for an eight week period starting in May. Known for its topical films, Warner Bros. was in a quandary. The headlines weren't so hot, but credit must be given to them for not shying away from difficult subjects.

The Mayor of Hell with James Cagney and Madge Evans-1933.

The Mayor of Hell was given a budget of $229,000, which was an average production budget at the studio during this time. The original story cost only $2,500, with another $3,370 spent for the treatment. Frankie was paid $250 per week. The filming commenced on Jan. 23, 1933 under the direction of Archie Mayo. Frankie endured some particularly long days of filming. On March 3, they worked from 9 am until 1:01 am and then five days later they worked from 10 am until 2:14 am. Long days for Frankie who was only fifteen years old at the time.

Filming wrapped on March 18 under the direction of Michael Curtiz, who shot the last two days of production.

The film opens with a gang of street kids offering to "watch over" parked cars just to make sure that nothing happens to them. The kids are led by Jimmy (played by Frankie). When a car owner refuses the insurance offer, the kids let the air out of his tire and steal his radiator cap. Later, when the gang attempts to steal some candy from a neighborhood shop, Frankie punches out the proprietor, sending him crashing through a glass display case. The kids are eventually caught by the police at their hangout and wind up in front of a judge for sentencing. We get a glimpse of the parents of some of the kids, who seem for the most part sorely lacking in parental acumen. When Frankie and his father approach the bench, his father snarls to Frankie, "I'll fix you for getting me in here." Frankie snaps back, "Why? You didn't have any place to go."

Most of the kids end up in reform school run by a sadistic warden named Thompson (played with relish by Dudley Diggs). Thompson runs a hellhole of a reform school, which features whippings, food not fit for an animal and barbaric solitary confinement. Things are running just fine for Thompson until one day, small time hoodlum and ward healer Patsy (played by James Cagney) arrives. Patsy has been made a deputy commissioner as a political favor. Patsy falls in love with the school nurse Dorothy (played by Madge Evans). Dorothy eventually thaws Patsy's rough exterior, and then Patsy, realizing how horrible the kids are treated, starts a reform movement. First he removes warden Thompson and takes over the position himself. He then sets up a democratic system of justice for the kids to follow. Then Patsy has to take it on the lam after he's involved in a justifiable shooting.

Thompson returns to the school and reestablishes his reign of cruelty. The kids, who were beginning to enjoy life under Patsy, revolt after the return of Thompson. The revolt is getting out of hand when Patsy arrives back at the school to reinstate his brand of social order.

As said before, Frankie is given only sixth billing, but he is the true star of the film. The players listed above him in the credits are all Warner contract players. Even *Variety* took note of Frankie's performance this time, noting in its review, "Element of interest for the box office is the 250 or so boys who participate in the picture. Particularly Frankie Darrow (sic). He's one of the leaders...Darrow and Dudley Diggs cop important attention." An east coast review in the *Journal*, written a few days after the film's opening on July 1, 1933 called Frankie, "an expert young actor."

As the film opens, Frankie's character shows no redeeming social values. He smashes the shop-keeper on the jaw with humorless determination. He's quick to show the gang that he's in charge, and at the same time he takes charge of the film itself. Top billed Cagney does not appear in the film for the first twenty-five minutes. It's a tribute to Frankie's skill as an actor, that when Cagney does finally arrive on the screen you don't think to yourself "It's about time!" Frankie is in such control of the film that you say to yourself, "Oh, I forgot Cagney is in the film". Cagney disappears from the film toward the finale, only to reappear to wrap things up in the final seven minutes. Again, the viewer doesn't mind because it has become Frankie's film. Unfortunately, as good as Frankie is, the script does not do the story justice. Cagney's character changes from a tough to reform minded do-gooder in nothing flat. The film does not really need someone as dynamic as Cagney in what should have been a supporting role. At the time Frankie was starting to be compared with Cagney. While the film was in production, Frankie stated to the press that he considered Cagney one of his best friends. Being that it's Frankie's first major role at an A studio, it's also a shame that he could not work with Cagney again as they work so well together here.

Warner Bros. must have liked the story. They dusted off the script and reworked it not once, but twice for The Dead End Kids, first in 1938 as *Crime School*, then in 1939 as *Hell's Kitchen*. Humphrey Bogart would play the Cagney role in the first remake and Ronald Reagan in the second.

Not being a studio contract player would have its pluses and minuses for Frankie and for his career. On the plus side he couldn't be shoved in any part in any film at Warner's behest. This action caused many of the biggest stars at Warner to jump ship the first chance they could get. On the downside, Warner's had no compunction to find the best parts for someone not in its stable of players. Perhaps more importantly, not being under a regular studio contract, Frankie wasn't being paid a salary unless he was actually working on a film.

Frankie lucked out with his next film at Warner's. William Wellman (who directed Frankie in *The Public Enemy)* gave Frankie a starring role in his upcoming feature *Wild Boys of the Road.*

On March 4, 1933 Franklin Delano Roosevelt was elected the President of the United States. With the arrival of the New Deal and The National Recovery Act, hope was running high that the end of the Great Depression was at hand. "Prosperity was just around the corner" was the catch phrase of the day. Unfortunately, life was still difficult for the vast majority of Americans. Wellman wanted to show just how hard life could be for some of the most vulnerable Americans, the children.

As mentioned before, it was not uncommon for Warner's or Wellman for that matter, to produce films from the headlines of the daily newspapers. *I Was a Fugitive From A Chain Gang, Two Seconds,* and Wellman's *Heroes For Sale* were stories about the nature of society that few, if any, other studios would dare touch. *Wild Boys of the Road* was based on newspaper accounts of the thousands of youth who, due to dire economic conditions, who were forced to leave their homes in search of a better life elsewhere.

Wild Boys of the Road with Dorothy Coonan and Edwin Phillips-1933.

In *Wild Boys of the Road*, Wellman cast Frankie in the lead (as Eddie Smith) along with Dorothy Coonan (as Sally) and Edwin Philips (as Tommy). During preproduction, while casting was still in progress, Frankie happened to be in Wellman's office when Dorothy Coonan arrived for her audition. While waiting for the director, she expressed her nervous trepidation over the audition to Frankie. She had never had more than a bit part in movies, and now she was up for the female lead. Both were sitting on a couch, and Frankie put his arm around her, drew her close to him and said blissfully, "Don't worry about a thing, the director is a friend of mine." At that instant, Wild Bill enters the room, sees Frankie, and yells "Get your hands off my girl!" Unbeknownst to Frankie they had been dating. Wild Bill had spotted Dorothy roller skating around the studio when she was between scenes on *Gold Diggers of 1933*, and they began dating shortly there after.

Frankie and Frank Sr. had moved to 1626 N. Serrano Ave., located between Hollywood Blvd. and Sunset Blvd. by the time the film was to commence. Frankie was paid $250 per week for the four week shoot. Co-star Dorothy Coonan was paid only $100 a week. Director Wellman received $24,000 for his work on the film. Warners paid out $3,519.74 for the story, and another $7,077.12 for the treatment. The film's total budget was $176,000. The film was based on an original story by Danny Ahearn entitled *Desperate Youth*.

Trouble arose when a writer named Wallace Sullivan threatened a lawsuit against Warner Bros. claiming he had written a similar story. Sullivan had pulled this before with Warners on *Picture Snatcher*, but to move the production along, they paid him $875 and gave him fifteen minutes to pitch an idea for a possible film starring James Cagney or Edward G. Robinson.

Warner Bros. had high hopes for the film. Producer and later actor Raymond Griffith wrote to production executive Hal Wallis on April 26, 1933 stating, "I think this, if well directed, has the opportunity of being one of the years outstanding pictures." He was correct in his assumption. Production began on Saturday June 17, 1933 at 8:45 am. The first scene shot was the dance inside the high school auditorium. Filming wrapped for the day at 11 pm. Filming continued six days a week until July 20 when filming wrapped. The final sequence shot was the interior of Aunt Carrie's apartment.

The film opens very deceptively. The local high school is having a dance, and Frankie and his pal Tommy (played by Edwin Phillips) arrive to the dance with their two dates in Frankie's convertible. Tommy is intertwined with his date in the back seat when he complains, "I've never seen a woman like this-all she wants to do is kiss." The girl responds with, "Slow poke!" This reminds us it's a pre-code Warners film, not a regulation "kids in high school" film. The kids open the door and get out of the car, all except Frankie, of course, who does his normal (for him anyway) leap over the door and into the street. The car is painted with various slogans and has an anchor. This could almost be the opening of an Andy Hardy film, if they were making them at the time. Tommy is broke, so the group sneaks him in dressed as a girl, since girls are admitted free. Later, on their way home, Frankie asks Tommy why he refused his offer to drive downtown. Tommy admits that his mom can't find a job and that they are getting their food from the Community Chest. Frankie offers to ask his father to help Tommy's mother because he's positive his father could get her a job at the cement company where he is working. At this point in the film the plot seems pretty well set, but it takes a sharp turn when Frankie arrives home. Upon entering the kitchen, Frankie grabs a big piece of pie but moments later hears his parents having a serious discussion in the other room. Frankie's look is heartbreaking. It turns out that his father has lost his job. When his father, after days of looking for work, still is unemployed, Frankie sells his beloved car for $22 and gives the money to his father. When the family's economic condition looks hopeless, Frankie has an idea.

He tells Tommy that they can hitch a ride on a train, travel to another town and get jobs to help out their families. Without consulting anyone, they leave a note for their parents and take to the trains. Once aboard a flatcar, they meet up with what they believe is another boy. Frankie gets in a fight with "him" over a missing sandwich, and Frankie gets his nose bloodied. The "boy" turns out to be Sally (played by Dorothy Coonan). The trio is complete. They head to Chicago to meet Sally's aunt. For a moment life is looking a little less bleak when they are greeted by Aunt Carrie (played by Minna Gomber). However, once inside the apartment, viewers realize even if the kids don't-that she is running a brothel.

The three just have time to sit down at the kitchen table to have a bite of chocolate cake when the place is raided by the police. Once again it's back to the rails. Their ranks swell to such an extent that the kids, who now number in the hundreds, are able to fight off the railroad police with a barrage of eggs. While the egg fight ensues outside, a railroad worker named Red (played by Ward Bond) is making advances on one of the young girls named Grace (played by the underused Rochelle Hudson). Grace, believing she is alone in the railroad car, removes her sweater to dry it off over a small fire. Clad in her bra, she is spotted by Red, who enters the car. She quickly puts her sweater back on. Red offers to dry it out in the caboose. She refuses, and Red makes a grab for her breast. Again she rebuffs his advances, and Red closes the door of the boxcar. When the kids, led by Frankie, return to the car, Frankie notices that something is wrong with her. She tells Frankie what happened. Red peeks his head through an opening in the roof and demands to know who broke into the refrigerator car. "I did," snarls Frankie. The huge Red climbs into the car to take care of Frankie but instead is attacked by the mob of kids. He's tossed out of the moving car, which happens to be going over a trestle at the time. The kids make an escape off the moving train before it arrives at the next station. Tommy, in jumping from the moving train, crashes into a railroad sign and is knocked unconscious, landing on a railroad track in the path of an oncoming locomotive. Tommy tries to move out of the way, but the train runs over one of his legs. Frankie locates a doctor for his wounded pal. In an intense and frightening scene, Tommy's leg is removed by the doctor. The boys, who still number in the hundreds, have taken up residence in Cincinnati at a sewer pipe manufacturing plant. They use the huge pipes as makeshift homes. Kids of all ages have come together in an almost blissful existence. It's not long until the authorities arrive and use high pressure water hoses to clean out the area.

Frankie, along with Tommy and Sally, wind up living at a dump in New York City. Life is still difficult, but Frankie gets a lead for a job. All he needs is a pair of blue pants and an alpaca coat. All three hit the street to raise the required money. Sally tap dances to Tommy's harmonica playing, and Frankie makes a deal with a couple of sharpies to deliver a note to the cashier at a movie theater. The note turns out to be a demand for money. The cashier screams, and Frankie makes a mad dash into the theater. The cops are in quick pursuit and capture Frankie inside the theater. All three kids wind up in before of a judge. After, soulful consideration, the judge agrees to find work for the trio so that they can raise enough money to return to their respective homes. Once outside the courthouse, Sally asks Frankie if he is happy. "I'll show you how happy I am," Frankie answers. Frankie does four back flips, then spins on his head then he gives a sympathetic look when he realizes that his friend Tommy would be unable to perform such a feat, he pats his friend on the shoulder, they get into a car with an official from the court and the story ends.

Wild Boys of the Road is the perfect showcase for Frankie's talents. From the light-hearted opening scenes of comedy, to the dramatic amputation scene, to his free spirit head spin at the finale, Frankie shows he's in command and can easily take the lead in an A picture.

Wellman insisted on filming on natural locations, which helps to give the film an almost documentary look. Extensive location work was done at the American Concrete Pipe Company at 4635 Firestone Boulevard in South Gate California, along with the Columbus Freight Yard in Burbank, and in nearby Glendale where the exterior shots of Frankie's home was done. Filming in the studio was the preferred method in the early days of sound. It was much easier to control the sound recording. Wellman makes wonderful use of sound in the movie, especially the noise of the trains. His use of natural sound also adds to the documentary feel of the film.

Wellman finished the film on time, but the film ran over budget to the tune of $27,000, bringing the final cost to $203,000.

One must credit Warner Bros. with the audacity to produce such a frequently bleak film during the Great Depression. During production in late July there was talk among the executives at Warners about placing Frankie under a long term contract. On one interoffice memo it stated that Frankie's father was asking as much as $1,750 a week for a fifty two week contract for his son's services. For whatever reason, no long term contract was ever signed. Before the film release in late 1933 the film ran into censorship problems. Censor boards in Ohio and Pennsylvania protested the film as did Australia and Quebec. The censor board in Quebec suggested tacking on a prologue to remind the audiences that this is all taking place in the United States, and not Canada! Warner Bros. released the film just in time to beat the strict production code that would take hold the following year.

Upon release, on October 7, 1933 the film received mostly raves from the critics. In its review *Variety* called the film, "a powerful and graphic social document" but it also added, "fact is that it makes for a depressing evening in the theater." Without Frankie's powerhouse performance, and to a slightly lesser degree Dorothy Coonan's, it could have become a very depressing film. You just know that with Frankie leading the group, life would turn out well somehow.

In his *Variety* review Rush, singled out Frankie for praise, stating "Young Frankie Darro turns in a first rate job as a spunky young tramp," and then mistakenly states, that this was Frankie's "first principle assignment, although he has been seen in numerous bits." Apparently Rush was never assigned to review Mascot films. Richard Watts, Jr. an east coast film critic raved about Frankie's performance, "It is (WILD BOYS) immeasurably aided, too, by the performance in the leading role of that genuinely brilliant boy actor Frankie Darrow (sic)." He wrapped up his positive review with, "This young Frankie Darrow (sic) really is one of the first-rate actors of the screen and in *'WILD BOYS OF THE ROAD'* he does marvels in adding a quality of mingled bitterness and gentleness to his part." Some of the reviews noted the similarity in plot to the Russian film *The Road of Life*, an account of homeless wandering Russian children, most preferring the Russian film, but they all seemed to enjoy Frankie's performance.

Another unknown east coast critic writing in the *Mirror*, opened the review with, "Frankie Darro, a youngster and a great actor, gives an overwhelming performance in this exciting and harrowing melodrama" Frank S. Nugent in his review of Sept. 22, 1933 touched on an aspect that would be a sore point for William Wellman the rest of his life, "by ending it with a happy ending, the producers have robbed it of its value as a social challenge." Wellman regretted having to use a happy ending. There were in fact three separate endings filmed. During production on July 19, Wellman filmed two different endings for the film.

One ending had the trio sentenced to reform school. The other was called "the happy ending." After the production had wrapped Wellman gathered his three youthful costars together again on August 7 and shot the courtroom scene again. It is the ending used in the finished film. Having the trio tossed into a reform school might have worked on a "social challenge" level, but not as entertainment. To spend sixty-six minutes with these resourceful kids, only to have them wind up behind bars, would be the ultimate in depressing movie going, especially during 1933. This was not a period film after all, it was the Great Depression. The original story had Frankie's character up on murder charges at the finale, the "happy" twist was that the charges are reduced to manslaughter!

Wellman would always rate the film high on his best ten list. Perhaps in part because a few months after the film's release, the four times wedded director married Dorothy Coonan. It would be a happy marriage, and it would last until 1976, when he died at age of 79. It would remain an important film for Dorothy Coonan as well. She made only a few other film appearances after her marriage, but she was justifiable proud of *Wild Boys of the Road*. When asked about Frankie and the making of the film, some seventy years after its release she looked wistfully aside and said, "Frankie, he was so talented."

Frankie considered *Wild Boys of the Road* his best film. Until his death he would keep a newspaper stuffed away that he would gladly pull out and show to guests. The front page showed the premiere of *Wild Boys of the Road*, and the huge crowd surrounding the movie theater.

Wild Boys of the Road was pretty much forgotten until it started popping up at William Wellman retrospectives in the early 1970's. When it was shown in Hollywood in May of 1974, Wellman and

Dorothy both showed up at the screening. If Frankie was invited, he didn't show. The film has never been released on home video. It was announced for release on laser disc, but the format died out before it was released. With the advent of cable TV, it started showing up on TBS, and later on TCM, which now plays the film with great frequency.

The saddest aspect of all this is that Frankie was not able to parlay this wonderful showcase of his talents into another starring part at Warner Bros. At the time, Warners was not making films starring young kids. It wouldn't be until "The Dead End Kids" arrived some five years later that they would see the importance of younger stars.

Seven months after the release of *Wild Boys of the Road*, Frankie was back in a supporting role in *The Merry Frinks*. Billed seventh, he plays Norman Frink. With his slicked back greasy hair, he plays the family's insolent son, talking back to everyone, including his old gray haired grandmother. In fact he even goes so far as to toss a newspaper in her face. The theme of the film is rather close to the play *You Can't Take It With You*, which would be playing on Broadway two years later. Besides Frankie's comic turn, Warner's contract player Allen Jenkins is hilarious as the communist loving lawyer of the family. One of the side plots involves Frankie becoming a boxer, and he comes up with the name Stinky Frink. He does a funny comic snort with his nose when he announces his choice of a name to his family. The reviews for the film were harsh. *Variety* went so far as to say, "It's strictly a machine-made product, offering the most disagreeable family since *Three Cornered Moon*."

At the time, a film with such a dysfunctional family must have seemed out of place and off putting. However, some seven decades after its initial release, it comes across as a fast paced and very funny movie.

By 1935 Warner's economic woes were just about over. They would hit the jackpot with films as diverse as *Gold Diggers of 1935* and *Captain Blood*. By years end the studio would show a profit of $674,158.

Frankie's next film for Warner's was entitled *Red Hot Tires*, and was released in February 1935. Frankie, fourth billed this time, plays an auto mechanic named Johnny. The car race drama takes a dramatic turn when ace driver and all around good guy Wallace Storm (played by Lyle Talbot), is accused of murder. Wallace flees the country, winding up in South America, where he becomes a famous race car driver under an assumed name. Wallace returns to the States for a big race and is about to be discovered when Frankie saves the day by fingering the real killer.

Frankie and Mary Astor in *Red Hot Tires*-1935.

The film would have been better with a stronger leading man. Talbot would become a dependable supporting player in years to come, but he was not the take charge guy the film needed. At the scant running time of fifty-six minutes, it more than met the requirements of a fast paced time filler.

Four months later in June 1935, Warner's released *Stranded.* Starring Kay Francis and Frankie's pal from Mascot, George Brent, who was working his way up the ladder of stardom at Warner's. By the time of the film's release, Francis and Brent had become something of a screen team, having appeared in six films together. The film concerns the building of the Golden Gate Bridge and the love life of the builder Mack (played by Brent) who is wooing an employee of the Traveler's Aid Society, Lynn (played by Francis). Frankie, billed way down in the twelfth spot plays Jimmy Rivers. Frankie was paid $400.00 a week for his work on the film. *The New York Times* gave the film a slightly positive review, citing, "[that] the picture's chief virtue is its sense of humor." The film is ably directed by Frank Borzage, at the time a well respected director.

Frankie's final film for Warner's of this period was entitled *The Payoff,* released in November 1935. In the film sportswriter Joe McCoy (played by James Dunn) writes an expose of gangster Autry Buhler's (played by Alan Dinehart) penchant for fixing sporting events. Joe's wife Maxine (played by Claire Dodd) befriends the gangster and eventually becomes his mistress. Joe winds up as a drunk in a waterfront saloon. Joe's friend, jockey Jimmy Moore (played by Frankie, of course) tells the down and out scribe about the fix Buhler has put on the big race. Joe sobers up and writes an expose of the race implicating Buhler in the fix. During the race itself, Frankie pulls his horse ahead of the pack and is shot for trying to win the race. He is fading fast but manages to stay on and win the race. With the expose published just as the race finishes, Joe gets his job back at the paper and winds up with coworker Connie (played by Patricia Ellis) who has loved him all along.

It may have been just another jockey role for Frankie, but his part was integral to the plot. Frankie's character starts out as a newspaper boy who tells McCoy at one point, "I'm going to be a jockey someday." Frankie is billed sixth and receives a nice photo credit as well. It's almost a cliché to say the film was a fast paced Warner production, as so many were in this period. However, this film seems faster paced than usual. The film is well edited, with no wasted footage. The film's authentic feel is perhaps due to the original story and co-screenplay being written by long time New York newspaper man George Bricker.

Director Robert Florey should also be credited with keeping the story moving at such a rapid pace. In its review *Film Daily* noted that "production turns out to be highly satisfying entertainment for the regular run of fans." *Variety* stated it was "another success item with romantic angles, but in both story and production it's much better than some Dodd has recently made."

The most amazing aspect of the film is that it crams all these twists and turns into a scant sixty-four minute running time.

Frankie's years at Warner Brothers offered him his shot at mainstream stardom. Warner's was a class A studio that offered all the benefits an actor at the time could ask for. Unfortunately, for Frankie the stardom didn't occur. He did of course make the near classic *Wild Boys of the Road* there, and if for no other film, his years at Warner Bros. were worthwhile.

CHAPTER 6
THE BIG CONN

It was spring of 1934 and the Great Depression raged on. Unemployment was a whooping 23.5% and the average wage was only $1,368 a year. Frankie's father had his son convinced that they were wealthy and had money squirreled away in numerous banks. Frankie was very much in demand as an actor, even though the demands for his talents were mostly from producers of B films. Yes, life was good for the Darros during the depths of the Great Depression. Soon it would get a little better.

Maurice Conn had a plan. As comptroller and assistant to the president of Mascot Pictures, he had watched his boss Nat Levine make the big bucks grinding out B's for the unsophisticated rural audiences. He would soon get his chance. Like Levine, Conn was well versed in the art of film exhibition. He had started out in the film business with the Olympia and Sterling movie theater chains, and now he wanted a crack at production.

Conn set up his production offices at the Talisman Studios, located at 4516 Sunset Blvd. The studio was originally called The Reliance-Majestic Studios. It was the studio used by D.W. Griffith when he was filming *The Birth of a Nation* back in 1915. It was a well used studio. Talisman was a popular studio for many independent producers of the time. It was just the proper spot for the low budget independent producer as it saved a lot of money just renting production space on an as needed basis. Conn wouldn't have and didn't need the overhead that his former boss had. At the time, it was written that Conn started his producing career with a mere $250 in his pocket.

Since westerns were always an easy sell, not to mention inexpensive to produce, Conn hired the brother of popular western star Ken Maynard for a series of "oaters". Kermit Maynard might not have been the star that Ken was at the time, but at least he had some name recognition, which was a valuable commodity even then. Hoping to cash in with the action crowd, he hired former Mascot star Frankie for a series of ten "action-mellers," the parlance used at the time to describe that type of film. Later, Conn would hire Pinky Tomlin for a series of musicals, but Maynard and Frankie were his stars for the time being.

For independent B films of the era, especially the early entries, the Darro series, was quite good. The early films usually took place at some large-scale existing exterior locations such as an oil field or racetrack, which would lend a touch of class to the low budget productions. Many B films of the era were shot on cheap-looking interior sets as that not only saved money on location filming but made sound recording easier.

With the Great Depression sapping the strength out of the nation, movie going was almost a necessity. To escape the dreary realities of life, audiences lined up at the box office, where escape from the hard times could be had for a nickel. With his Darro series, Conn delivered the escapist goods. The films might look quaint some seventy years later, but they were just the things for audiences of the period and remained so for years eventually winding up with constant showings during the early days of television. Conn sold the films on a state rights' basis. Not having a distribution network like the major studios, he sold his films outright to regional distributors. The films could then be rented by these distributors until the prints themselves wore out. Then they would simply buy more prints from Conn.

Frankie's series was kicked off on July 13, 1935 with the release of *Men of Action*. The story concerns a vicious banker (were there ever any other kind in the movies?) played by bad guy stalwart, Fred Kohler. The evil banker is sabotaging the building of a dam. Without the dam valuable farm land will be rendered useless. Frankie is given less screen time in this initial entry than would be the case for the rest of the series. Frankie plays the son of a farmer who was killed by the banker's cohorts. Frankie has a touching crying scene when he learns of his father's death.

While the scene is effective and touching. Frankie would have an even better similar scene the following year in *Black Gold*. Frankie was always given an adult costar in the series to handle the love interest, and often, act as a surrogate father. Roy Mason (also known as Leroy Mason) would handle the assignment in the first three films.

The exterior location filming helps the film, but the lack of musical score makes the film seem less than exciting today. It was, however, a good introduction to the series, with even better entries to follow.

Roy Mason on Frankie's right in *Men of Action* -1935.

Valley of Wanted Men was up next, released on October 23, 1935. Roy Mason plays a convict who escapes from prison to clear his name on a false bank robbery charge. Mason makes his way to a mountain resort in an effort to find the real thief and in turn finds out that his ex-girlfriend is about to marry the real crook. Frankie plays Slivers Sanderson, an old buddy of Mason, who helps him not only capture the bad guy but, of course, helps him get his girl back. As with most of the entries, it was based on a story by Peter B. Kyne, entitled "All For Love". Kyne, a popular San Francisco based writer at the time, is probably best remembered today for his often filmed story "The Three Godfathers". *Valley of Wanted Men* has just about all one could ask for in a mid 30's B film. The outdoor location filming at Lake

Arrowhead, California is a big plus, Lake Arrowhead was a popular destination for vacationing actors in the 1930's.

Frankie is as energetic as ever in the film. He does a wonderful rear horse mount, virtually flying into the saddle with his customary ease. The prison shoot-out that opens the film is unusually violent. It's amazing that Mason and his two accomplices actually make it through the hail of machine gun fire, as no one else seems to. Future popular character actor Paul Fix essays an early role as one of the escaped convicts. On the minus side is the appearance of an actor who went by the stage name of Snowflake, (in reality Fred Tonnes).

Mr. Tonnes is one of a handful of African-American actors who were given demeaning, subservient roles at the time and for the most part portrayed their characters as dimwitted boobs. Snowflake would pop up in various entries during the run of the series. Fortunately, he doesn't have much to do this time around. Retakes were a luxury on most B films of the time. Producers depended on actors like Frankie who could deliver their dialogue on the first take without flubs. Perhaps they didn't think that anyone would notice, or perhaps the director or Conn himself didn't notice, but in one scene while he's tending bar someone actually refers to Snowflake as Snowball!

Shortly before his eighteen birthday in December 1935, Frankie stepped before the cameras to film the third entry in the series, *Black Gold.* The black gold of the title is, of course oil. Frankie's father is the owner of an oil field and has just thirty days to find oil or lose his field to the finance company. Frankie's father is killed by the crooks working for the finance company. Roy Mason, an undercover government agent, tries to help Frankie and his sister run the field and discover oil before the deadline. Oil is struck at the end when the crooks set off a series of explosions intent on destroying the field. The explosions inadvertently set off a gusher of oil.

The basis of the film was another Peter B. Kyne story, "The Joy of Living", that appeared in Popular Magazine on February 1, 1914. Kyne was so popular at the time that his name was billed above the titles on most of the Conn films, something Frankie had yet to achieve. Frankie plays a character named Clifford "Fishtail" O'Reilly. Frankie's athletic ability is really on display this time around. At one point in the film Frankie is sitting at his desk in a school room when he becomes bored with the lesson he makes a perfect running dive out the open window. His dramatic ability is also well utilized.

At the beginning of the film, Frankie watches in horror while his father falls to his death due to sabotage on an oil derrick. The film's director, Russell Hampton, wisely lets the scene play silent. As Frankie approaches his dead father, the screen is filled with a close-up of Frankie's face, and it slowly fills with the look of horror. The scene is vivid and effective.

The director is also in the cast, he plays Anderson, the villain who is the head of the finance company. A big plus this time is the location. Filming at an actual oil field in Newhall, 20 miles north of Los Angeles, effectively adds to the film's authenticity. The extras were real oil workers who were paid $3.50 a day to play themselves. Some of the extras were actually injured when the crew was testing the explosives to be used in the finale. The test blast unexpectedly blew lumber over a large area that was to be used for filming. No one was seriously injured and Frankie had not yet arrived on the set. Creative use of optical wipes, widely used at the time, is also a big plus. As good as the film is, it's somewhat hampered by the appearance of Snowflake again. While Frankie is never demeaning in his attitude toward him, he shows none of the camaraderie that would be so important a few years later when he performed with Mantan Moreland. The film, running a scant fifty-eight minutes, was released on Dec. 20, 1935.

Born to Fight was the next entry in the series, released on April 17, 1936. With this film Conn made a major casting change. He replaced Roy Mason with Kane Richmond. The lanky six foot Richmond would remain in the series to the finish. Richmond was born in Minneapolis, Minnesota on December 23, 1906. He had started out as a film booker for the state's rights business before deciding to cross over to acting. Richmond did not possess the easygoing charm of Mason, and he was a little uncomfortable delivering dialogue in the early entries, but he did become more competent as the series wore on. It should also be noted that he made a great action hero in the 1940 Republic serial *Spy Smasher*. The plot of *Born to Fight* has Richmond as a champion boxer who's on the lam for cold cocking a mob boss (played by Jack Larue). While at a hobo encampment Richmond meets up with Frankie and trains him in his unique style of boxing. Larue eventually finds out that Richmond is behind the quickly rising fame of featherweight Frankie. Larue forces Frankie to attempt to throw the championship fight, until the pleading of Richmond ringside convinces Frankie to do otherwise. Frankie winds up winning the championship. Up to his ears in fight debts he cannot possibly pay off, Larue exits the fight arena and takes the coward's way out by shooting himself. Off camera, of course. *Born to Fight* is one of the best entries in the series. Frankie plays it in a more subdued way than usual and it works out well. He uses very little of the "Gee" or "Golly Gee" dialogue, that was so prevalent in the previous entries. Frankie's introduction at a hobo camp is reminiscent of *Wild Boys of the Road,* only this time he's off the road rather quickly. The plot is more complex than usual. There are two concurrent story lines, which help keep the film running at a brisk pace. Frankie is a joy to watch in the ring. He's so full of energy that he leaps straight up while boxing his opponent. With his shirt off, his well toned torso gives him the look of a real boxer. The film itself has a polished production look, and with liberal use of exterior locations, it has a style much like that of a big studio production. Conn has done himself proud with this entry. Even *Variety*, which was pretty tough on the series, liked the film, stating, "It will please fight fans and will round out double bills very nicely as a better than average film of its kind."

Four months later, on August 13, 1936 Conn released the next feature in the series, *Racing Blood.* In this film Frankie buys a lame colt from friend and breeder Kane Richmond. Frankie nurses it back to health and enters it in the big race. Yes, it wins, but not before Frankie's brother Smokie, a jockey, is framed for betting on the races. Frankie clears his brother's name at the finish. A rather weak entry, the movie is based on the Kyne story "Lionized". The cinematography is sloppy, and one has to contend with Arthur Houseman playing one of his "funny drunk" characters again. Unfortunately, he's nowhere near as humorous as he was so often in the Laurel and Hardy shorts in which he appeared.

Conn waited eight months to release the next film in the series. *Headline Crasher* made its debut on April 6, 1937. Frankie moves up on the social ladder in this entry. He plays the son of a United States Senator. Frankie is accused of being an accomplice in a robbery during his father's reelection campaign. A gangster named Scarlotti, newly released from prison, plans to kill the Senator because it was the Senator, who as a district attorney sent him to prison in the first place. At the conclusion, Scarlotti holds Frankie, Richmond and Muriel Evans hostage at the senator's mountain retreat. Frankie saves the day by disarming the bad guys.

Frankie and Richmond start out as adversaries in this one. Richmond plays a reporter out to dig up dirt on the senator. He changes his tune as he falls in love with the senator's secretary (played by Muriel Evans). The film is helped enormously by the exterior filming in the sparsely populated San Fernando Valley. The opening airport sequence was filmed at the Glendale Grand Central Air Terminal, a frequently used film location. Also a plus for the film is the stronger than usual female role for the series. Instead of just hanging around waiting for Kane Richmond to fall in love with her, Muriel Evans shows some spunkiness when dealing with the villains. Evans is probably best remembered for the series of eight Charlie Chase shorts she did in 1932, as well as her early B westerns. Frankie is as agile as ever this time around. He flies through the air during a fight scene and effortlessly jumps over the edge of a table as if gravity simply does not apply to him. During one chase scene, while trying to capture some of the bad guys, Frankie leaps for a tree limb and swings through the air, a la Tarzan. During the actual filming of the scene, the limb broke, and Frankie wound up on the camera crew instead. He was not injured and dusted himself off while the director, Les Goodwins, picked a stronger branch for the second take. Snowflake was replaced by Roy Martin this time. Martin was a professional football player from Chicago, and this was his first acting assignment. He plays a character named Martin. Unfortunately, his character is just as demeaning as any that Snowflake would play.

It was another solid entry all and all, but the only letdown is the sloppy ending. With one quick move Scarlotti is disarmed by Frankie, then Richmond confesses his undying love for Evans, and the film comes to an abrupt end. At the very least there should have been a good fight scene. *Variety* didn't like the film much, but they did state, "Frankie Darro is energetic as ever." *Film Daily* called it, "Good action meller [that] keep[s] churning out the thrills…" The pressbook, which is sent out to the theater owners to help with advertising, proposes a rather unusual way to sell the film. They suggest making up a poster to put in the lobby with a caption that would read, "Here are a few of today's *Headline Crashers*. They go on to suggest putting pictures in the lobby of local celebrities or citizens who happen to be in the news, they also state, "You might want to include newspaper photos of Wally Simpson, Hitler, King Edward or other internationally known publicity hounds." This is quite possibly the first time Adolph Hitler was ever used to sell a film. A news release done in conjunction with the film mentioned that Frankie was walking three times a week from his house in Beverly Hills to Griffith Park. He started this trek to cure a leg ailment, and even after it was cured he kept up the walk.

Tough to Handle was up next, released on May 25, 1937. The plot this time was pretty simplistic. Local gangster Franko (played by Harry Worth), is involved in a phony lottery ticket scam. Frankie's grandfather is the recipient of one of these phony tickets, which just so happens to have been imprinted with the matching number of the real ticket. When Frankie's grandfather is found dead in his apartment, Frankie and newspaper man Kane Richmond investigate and ultimately break up the racket. After six crackerjack entries, *Tough to Handle* is a bit of a let down. Unlike its predecessor, which used exterior locations to build the story around, *Tough to Handle* is filmed almost exclusively indoors on dull looking sets. The few exterior scenes are filmed mostly on the studio's streets. The film does have two worthwhile aspects however. Harry Worth does an excellent job as the oily gangster Franko who Frankie believes is his friend and benefactor. You can actually see the trepidation in Worth's face when he has to lie to his supposed friend (Frankie). The other plus is a wonderful dance routine performed by Frankie at Franko's nightclub. Frankie's sister (played by Phyllis Fraser) is trying to get a job there as a singer. Frankie tells her, "Hey, maybe we can do a brother and sister act." Then in a flash he moves to the dance floor and goes into a fantastic flip routine, first doing forward flips the whole length of the floor then doing back flips to where he began. For the finale Frankie spins on his head, as he did in *Wild Boys of the Road.* Without a break in the filming Frankie effortlessly delivers dialogue to his sister, not out of breath at all! The sequence is poorly cut, leaving Frankie off camera far too long, but it is a wonderful treat in a rather dull film. It's too bad this side of Frankie wasn't shown more often in films.

Variety dismissed the film as "unconvincing and slipshod," giving a positive spin only to Lorraine Hayes for her performance as Franko's girlfriend. It stated, "She shows promise and is worthy of better surroundings." Hayes dropped out of films shortly after the film was released.

Anything For a Thrill-1937.

Unfortunately, another weak entry was released just one month later on June 29, 1937. In *Anything for a Thrill* Frankie and Kane Richmond are a brother team of newsreel cameramen. A reclusive heiress by the name of Betty Kelly (played by popular model Ann Evers) purchases the business that employs them in an attempt to stop the cameramen from prying into her personal life. Unbeknownst to Kelly she's the target of a kidnap plot by a gang of crooks. Not a bad idea for a quickie B, but someone forgot about the plot halfway through the movie and it just seems to meander to its dull conclusion. It does have one highlight of sorts. During a scene in a projection booth, Richmond grabs playfully at Evers and inadvertently grabs her breast. It's quite obvious and for some reason was not cut out, as it easily could have been. It's a real surprise to a quick eyed film viewer.

Frankie with his screen partner Kane Richmond.

Frankie is given a love interest for the first time in the series, June Johnson plays his girlfriend, Jean Roberts. Roberts is constantly tagging along with the hesitant Frankie, as she wants more out of the relationship than Frankie. Johnson, daughter of Chic Johnson (half of the famed comedy team of Olsen and Johnson) plays the part like Gracie Allen. *Variety* really dismissed this entry, calling it an "incredible hoke adventure meller. For downstair doubles, if at all." A little rough perhaps, but not far off the mark!

Conn didn't waste any time in releasing the next entry, *Devil Diamond*, on June 30, 1937, just one month following the previous movie. The devil diamond of the title refers to a supposed cursed rock called the Jarvis diamond. A gang of crooks who posses the diamond plans to have it cut into smaller pieces for easy resale. The gang takes up residence in the quiet town of San Juan so that an unsuspecting retired diamond cutter can work on the diamond. Frankie plays an amateur boxer who is being used as a front to hide the diamond cutting operation. Incognito as a writer, Richmond is actually an insurance investigator, hot on the heals of the villains. The film is rather leisurely paced, especially for one running a scant sixty-one minutes.

Frankie is again given a reluctant love interest, but his actions toward the girl border on mean spiritedness, and you start feeling sorry for her in the way the script treats their relationship. Frankie gets involved in fights with the crooks that show him as spunky as ever. The finale features a slam bang car chase done on location without the use of the rear projection techniques that were generally used at the time. One of the poorest aspects of the film is its musical score. To save money Conn uses what sounds like public domain classical music. The score is so out of place it actually ruins some scenes. This is nowhere near the best of the series, but not the worst either. The worst would follow.

Realizing this would be the final entry in the series, Conn may have lost interest. *Young Dynamite*, released on December 15, 1937, is easily the poorest entry in the series. Even Peter B. Kyne is left behind this time. The film is based on the book "State Trooper" by Arthur Durlam. As filmed, it's not much of a story. With the United States off the gold standard, gangster Flash Slaven (played by William Costello) has a plan to hoard the rare ore for himself. Frankie's older brother (played by ace stuntman David Sharpe) is killed by gangsters. Frankie joins forces with neophyte trooper Kane Richmond to bust the gold racketeers. The film plays like one long chase but, unfortunately, not a very exciting one. The plot is full of unbelievable coincidences. At one point, Frankie just happens to meet up with the bad guys on a deserted road; another time the crooks are at a gas station when their description just happens to be broadcast over the radio for all to hear. Plot points happen just because they have to happen, not due to any dramatic sensibility. Sharp, who essays the brief role of Frankie's brother, would replace Frankie on the Red Skelton television show years later. Surprisingly, *Variety* didn't trash the film too badly; in fact it even singled out Frankie and Pat Gleason as standouts in the cast.

Maurice Conn announced a few month before the release of *Young Dynamite* that Frankie had signed a new long term contract with Conn Pictures Corporation. It was not to be however. *Young Dynamite* would be Frankie's last picture under the Conn banner because Conn Pictures would close up shop after its release. Conn would continue to produce the occasional B film for other studios such as Monogram and Eagle-Lion, but nothing he did was as ambitious as in his Conn Picture days. Maurice Conn died in Hollywood on October 16, 1973, largely forgotten, even by dyed in the wool film buffs.

Conn's ten films with Frankie are certainly not cinema classics, nor are they on par with the later films Frankie was to make at Monogram, but they are, for the most part, highly enjoyable B movies. They were made simply to entertain the audience for an hour, and they fulfilled that requirement admirably. For some odd reason the actual prints of the films seem to have weathered the ravages of time quite well. They look surprisingly sharp when viewed today, some seventy years later, especially for films that have long fallen into public domain. They are still highly enjoyable, with Frankie front and center, providing a bright spunkiness in the way that only Frankie could deliver.

CHAPTER 7
FIRST CALL JOCKEY
(RIDING TOWARD THE A FILMS)

Due to Frankie's height of 5'3", it's not surprising that he was fast becoming Hollywood's first choice for playing screen jockeys. Fortunately for Frankie, horse racing movies would be a staple of Hollywood for a long time to come.

He first rode atop a racehorse in the 1934 release *The Big Race*, an obscure independent film produced by Showmen's Pictures, Inc. The film concerns a racehorse owner trying to prove to his old man that he is not the crook that others believe him to be. The film starred the popular Boots Mallory. In its review for the film, *Variety* noted that it "lacks production finish…but on the whole offers fair entertainment as an indie." Frankie received fourth billing for his initial jockey role. The film would be re-released in 1951 as *King of the Race Track*.

Later that same year Frankie saddled up once more, this time for director Frank Capra, who had just directed the classic *It Happened One Night*. The new film entitled *Broadway Bill* starred Warner Baxter, who had portrayed Frankie's adopted father in *Amateur Daddy*. Frankie plays a crooked jockey this time out of the gate by the name of Ted Williams. It is a small part, as Frankie doesn't even show up until seventy minutes into the film. However, it did give him the opportunity to work with one of the major directors in Hollywood and at a studio that was rapidly becoming a major player in Hollywood, Columbia Pictures Corporation.

Frankie realized how important this was and considered working with Capra one of his best show business experiences. He also considered Capra one of the nicest men he would ever meet in the business. The film was not of the classic stature of Capra's previous release, but it's rousing fun most of the way. The film is beautifully shot by Joseph Walker and, like all of Capra's films, is populated by some of the best character actors in the business. Nobody could cast a film like Capra. Ace cinematographer Walker had shot *The Flying U Ranch* starring Tom Tyler and Frankie back in 1927. On the set of

Broadway Bill he reminded Frankie of an amusing story from the previous shoot. It seemed the director was having a problem lining up a shot of Tyler and Frankie racing on horseback. Frankie kept lagging behind, out of camera range. After several failed attempts Walker intervened and explained the problem to young Frankie. Frankie smiled and responded, "I know what I'm doing. If I stay back, you'll *have* to give me a separate close-up." Frankie laughed at the story, and added. "You'd better look out, Joe, I still do it!" During his brief appearance in the film, Frankie delivers his dialogue in a rather insolent manner. His playing of an arrogant crook must have been a shock to his fans who were used to his kid next door performances over at Mascot.

Columbia rehired Frankie for a non jockey role in their May 4, 1934 release of *No Greater Glory*. It would be Frankie's next try at a major role in an A film. The director, Frank Borzage, is virtually forgotten today but at the time was considered a top flight filmmaker with credits such as *Seventh Heaven* released in 1927 and *Young American Girl* in 1932, both garnering him Academy Awards for Best Director. *No Greater Glory* would be the closest Frankie would ever come to making what could be considered an art film. It is based on Ferenc Molnar's autobiographical novel "The Paul Street Boys," which had been filmed earlier in Germany. The story is told in metaphors and concerns two gangs of kids on the streets of Paris. The younger gang, The Paul Street Boys, are defending their turf (a lumberyard that they have rigged up as a fort) against a gang of older kids known as The Red Shirt Gang. When a gang war erupts, the battle is halted midstream by the death of Nemecsek, one of the Paul Street Boys. Nemecsek's death is caused by a lingering illness and not the gang war, but his death finally brings the boys from both feuding gangs together. After holding a makeshift funeral the boys learn that their disputed territory, the lumberyard, is to be turned into an apartment building. The character names are carried over from the novel. Frankie plays Feri Ats, leader of The Red Shirt Gang. Despite his second billing it is not a big part, nor is the film really a showcase for his talents. Frankie is more subdued than usual, but he does have a menacing presence, and when we see him for the first time we know he is trouble without Frankie having to speak a single line of dialogue. George P. Breakston has the important role of Nemecek, the young member of the Paul Street Boys.

If one can overlook some of the stilted acting in the lesser roles the film still holds a powerful anti-war message. In a sad and ironic turn of events, George P. Breakston was killed in battle eleven years later during World War II. The film was not a success for Columbia. The story was filmed again in 1969 as *The Paul Street Boys*.

Early in 1935 Frankie got another break from the jockey roles. For the first time in his career he went to work for Universal Studios. The film was entitled *Three Kids and a Queen* and starred May Robson. The plot was a twist on her Frank Capra directed hit of 1933, *Lady for a Day*. This time Robson is actually a rich woman, one of the richest in the world, the reclusive and mysterious Mary Jane "Queenie" Baxter. An accident leaves her suffering from amnesia, and she winds up being cared for by a character played by Henry Armetta and the three kids that he cares for. They all live together in Armetta's tenement apartment until gangsters discover Baxter's true identity, kidnap her and hold her for ransom. Frankie saves the day by leading the police to the gangsters' hideout. Frankie plays Blackie, one of the "Three Kids" on the title, the other two are played by future Bowery Boy Billy Benedict and Bill Burrud. Some of the movie's early exterior scenes are shot in front of a phony looking process screen, which tends to ruin the flow of the film, but on the whole it's a rather enjoyable film. Frankie gets a chance to sing a bit and dance, and he even does a few of his trademark double back flips during a routine with Benedict and costar Charlotte Henry. Frankie plays an effective dramatic scene with Robson when he has to have her sign a ransom note against her will. This makes her think that Frankie is not the good kid she always thought he was but, in fact, is in league with the kidnappers. It's not long before she learns her first impression was indeed correct after all. In a first for Frankie, he is given an adult love interest, albeit a young adult love interest. Charlotte Henry, a wonderful but woefully underused actress, plays the love interest he's planning to marry by the conclusion of the film.

Off-screen Frankie was considering marriage as well. His relationship with Virginia Gumm had turned serious about a year earlier. Virginia's father Fred had purchased a struggling five hundred seat theater in the high desert community of Lancaster, about sixty miles northeast of Los Angeles. Fred used the theater not only for vaudeville acts but to showcase his talented daughters. By the mid 1930's the theater had become successful and quite well known. Frankie, along with his Lawlor buddy Mickey Rooney, would frequently make the two hour drive up to Lancaster to see the girls perform. Frankie and Mickey would sometimes jump on stage and join in the show.

Besides giving Frankie a chance to appear in front of a live audience, it also gave him a chance to spend more time with Virginia, far away from the prying eyes of the Hollywood press corps. Frankie realized that his young fans did not want to hear about his involvement with girls, so he rarely spoke publicly about Virginia. The one time he did mention her in an interview, he spoke about her in terms of being a good friend, stating that he had no thoughts of marriage, but by the mid 1930's their relationship had turned very serious indeed. They had become engaged.

Columbia had raked in the profits on *Broadway Bill* so they returned to the racetrack the following year. On April 10, 1935 Columbia released *The Unwelcome Stranger*. The film stars Jack Holt and child actor Jackie Searl. Holt is a racehorse breeder who holds to a superstition that all orphans are unlucky, be it human or equine. Holt had been an orphan himself. His superstition forces him to almost sell his one prize racehorse and to snub the boy his wife wants to adopt. Frankie, billed seventh, plays Charlie Williams, a popular but crooked jockey. The ascot wearing Frankie is so mean and cynical, he even laughs at Searl when the boy asks him if prayers do any good. Frankie plays the role in a rather subdued way, but it is another fine performance in a role in which another actor could easily be forgotten. As fine as Frankie was in the role, it was unfortunately another jockey role, and he was not able to parley these fine performances into more substantial roles in important films.

By the mid 1930's Frankie was first call on the list of screen jockeys. While it gave him a source of income, it was not necessarily a good turn of events. It would begin to limit his appearances in A films to roles where he would be riding horses. By the time he was eighteen he was still only 5'3", too short of statue for adult roles but youthful looking enough to pass as a young teen.

On Sunday, November 17, 1935 Fred Gumm, the patriarch of the Gumm family, died of spinal meningitis. His estranged wife Ethel left her three daughters in the care of their neighbor, Dorothy Walsh, and Frankie. Ethel fled to the arms of her soon to be new husband Will Gilmore. The Gumm family home was now located at 842 North Mariposa Avenue, just south of Hollywood. The girls were too distraught over the death of their father to cook, so for the next three nights they sent Frankie out for hamburgers until their mother finally returned home. After Fred's passing Frankie and Virginia's friends assumed that the long planned wedding would finally take place.

It never did. The couple broke up, never to talk again, and the reason is lost to time. It could have been due to Frankie's ever increasing alcohol intake, not just at social occasions but daily and frequently enough to cause blackouts. Their breakup could also be due to the rumors that Frankie was having an affair with Virginia's sister Judy. For whatever the reason, Virginia ended up marrying musician Bobby Sherwood.

Toward the end of his life Frankie would look back on his romance with Virginia as one of the highlights of his life, the one that got away but stayed deep in his heart. Virginia dropped out of show business after her marriage and eventually passed away in Dallas, Texas on May 27, 1977.

With the release of *The Ex-Mrs. Bradford* on May 15, 1936, Frankie rode for the first time for a major studio. The film was released by RKO, the studio built on the ashes of Frankie's home studio during the silent film era (FBO). The stars of the film were William Powell and gravelly voiced Jean Arthur. The film plays like one of Powell's popular *Thin Man* movies, he was making over at MGM. Arthur plays Powell's ex-wife and bickering all the way, they solve a murder of a jockey. Frankie shows up during the final twenty minutes. It's the big race, and Frankie is prepping for his moment on the turf when, unbeknownst to him, the killer slips a black widow spider down the back of his silk, just before he is about to mount his horse. The spider bites him during the race, but it doesn't have the desired effect of killing him because just before the race Powell has given him a shot of anti-venom, disguised as a vitamin injection. Frankie does his own riding in the final race. The scene was filmed at Santa Anita, the popular race rack just south of Pasadena. Grant Mitchell, who portrayed Frankie's father in *Wild Boys of the Road*, appears here as John Sommers.

Later that same year Frankie saddled up again for *Charlie Chan at the Race Track* over at Twentieth Century Fox, generally considered one of the best Chan features produced by Fox. Frankie plays another crooked jockey, this time named "Tip" Collins. He takes a bride early on, only to foul the horse behind him. Frankie is "taken for a ride" about half way through the film, and the comment is made later that Collins was "fished out of the ocean off Santa Monica." Frankie's role in the film is more than just another jockey role this time. His character features prominently in the story until he is killed off of course. Frank Coughlin, Jr., Frankie's pal from *The Public Enemy* and *Mike,* also has a role as a jockey. The film is fast paced and has fine production values, thanks to being produced by a major studio. A few years hence the series would move to Monogram where the films would suffer due to lower budgets and shorter shooting schedules.

Early in 1937 Frankie was back at the crown jewel of movie studios, MGM. He was hired for a trio of A budget films. It gave Frankie yet another chance to break into A movies. He was a well established star of B films, but that was of little consequence. The A films were the respected ones. They were the movies released in the big theatres on the top of the bill, the ones that had the respect of the critics and fans. Unfortunately, all three films at MGM were jockey roles.

First was *A Day at the Races*, starring the Marx Brothers. The film was a follow up to their biggest hit. *A Night at the Opera*, released two years previous. Frankie had been a fan of their comedy antics since he had seen their first film, *The Coconuts*, in 1929. Frankie plays yet another crooked jockey. He's bad guy Morgan's ace in the hole during the big race. Morgan is played by popular bad guy actor Douglass Dumbrill, who worked with Frankie on *Broadway Bill* and later *Riding High* and *Lawless Rider.* Frankie doesn't show up until ninety-five minutes into the film, just in time to ride against Harpo in the big race. During the race Frankie strikes Harpo with a riding crop, much to Harpo's indignation. Frankie actually wins the race until it's discovered that the horses have been switched and Frankie has been riding the horse for the good guys all along. The racetrack scenes were again filmed at the beautiful Santa Anita Race Track.

The film as a whole is a pretty mixed bag. It's generally considered the last classic Marx Brothers film, but its laugh content is on the low side. It features lavish production numbers that do nothing for the plot or pace of the film. The plodding pace does finally pick up when the brothers finally make it to the racetrack. On Frankie's final day of work on the film, he brought an 11x14 portrait of the brothers to the set in order to have them autograph it for him. Groucho and Harpo gratefully obliged, but it took Frankie almost all day to track down the elusive Chico. It seems he was always away from the set making phone calls to his bookie, betting on real horse races. He finally did locate the comedian, who dutifully signed the portrait. Harpo would remain Frankie's favorite of all the brothers because he was always kind to him during the filming, something Frankie would remember for the rest of his life.

The following month, on July 2, 1937 MGM released *Saratoga*, another racetrack film that unfortunately has gone down in film history as the film that Jean Harlow was making when she died. The talented actress became ill during filming, but being the trooper she was, she pressed on. Sadly she died of uremic poisoning on June 7, 1937 before her scenes were completed. Viewing the film today, one can see her appearance changes from scene to scene. The toll the illness was taking on her body is quite obvious. She was doubled in a few scenes so the movie could be completed. Frankie unfortunately didn't get to work with her and never had the chance to meet her. Frankie plays Dixie Gordon, a jockey with the reputation of being the best rider on the circuit. He has a quick scene with Clark Gable at a pre-race party where, while smoking a cigar, he establishes his surly manner, which he carries throughout the film. Due to Harlow's death the film became a tremendous success and eventually became the highest grossing film of the year.

In August 1937 MGM began production on yet another horse racing saga entitled *Thoroughbreds Don't Cry*. The film marked the first paring of Frankie's pal Mickey Rooney and the sister of his fiancée, Judy Garland. The film was also slated to star Freddie Bartholomew. However, his voice started to change during preproduction so he was replaced by another lad from England, Ronald Sinclair. Rooney plays a bull headed famous jockey who agrees to throw a race to benefit his supposedly ill father. His crime is discovered before the race, and Rooney is banned from the track. As a last minute substitution for Rooney, Sinclair rides in his place. With some rapid off the track coaching by Rooney, Sinclair rides the horse to victory. Riding against Sinclair is Frankie, playing "Dink" Reid. Frankie is seen at the start of the film in a rooming house for jockeys. His character is humorless, and he's seen chomping on a cigar at the dinner table. He appears again during the final race. Frankie is at his surly best when warning Sinclair to stay away from him on the track. Sure, it's another crooked jockey role, but by this time Frankie had this type of character down pat. The film was released in November 1937. Rooney and Garland would go on to costar in another nine films. It would be Frankie's only film with both.

During his down time Frankie would play football with Rooney on the MGM Lions football team a team consisting of actors, technicians and others at the studio. Given all times that Frankie played jockeys on screen, one might think he actually enjoyed the sport, but this was not the case. He later stated that he could count the times he actually went to the track on one hand. Although he enjoyed riding horses, betting on them never interested him. Commenting on his many jockey roles he quipped, "I should have been paid by the mile."

Try as he might to make it into A films, Frankie resigned himself to the fact that A film stardom was beyond his reach, and he was simply happy to be working at a major studio. It must have been even more satisfying for him to realize that most of his early contemporaries were out of work. Even Shirley Temple's career was hitting the skids by the late 1930's. It has been stated over and over again-audiences just didn't want their child actors to grow up.

Early in 1938, Frankie had another shot at a major studio. Columbia Pictures hired him for two features and a serial. The first feature was entitled *Reformatory* and was released on July 21, 1938. It starred Columbia Pictures stalwart Jack Holt, along with Bobby Jordan, who was taking a break from his Dead End Kids films over at Warner's.

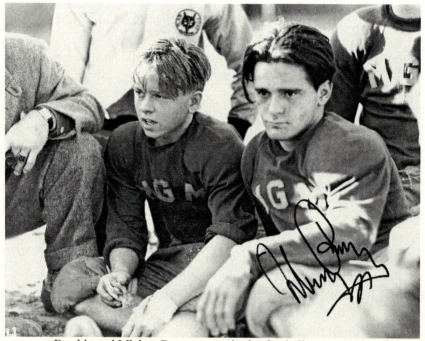

Frankie and Mickey Rooney at a charity football game-1938.

Holt plays the new reform minded warden of the Garfield State School. His appointment angers some in the system who are making a fine living from the reform school just the way it was always run in the past. To prove the new warden can't handle the job, one of the facility's ex-guards has tough kid Louis Miller (played by Frankie) transferred to Garfield, with orders to plan an escape. During the escape Miller drowns in a swamp. In the end, of course, Holt's brand of compassion turns the school from a cruel institution into an almost idyllic school for formally tough kids. Frankie received sixth billing. Sadly, the film is considered lost and as such, his performance cannot be evaluated.

Juvenile Court-1938.

On September 14, 1938 Columbia Pictures released *Juvenile Court*. The film features Paul Kelly and a pre-stardom Rita Hayworth, playing Frankie's sister. The casting plays better onscreen than it does in print. Frankie is billed third and plays the leader of a Dead End Kids type gang. They are seen baking mickeys (potatoes) over an open flame, just like the real Dead End Kids did in their first film. Kelly plays a District Attorney who sent Frankie and Rita's big bother to the death chamber. He now takes it upon himself to clean up the slums that breed the criminals. With his lightening fast delivery Frankie all but steals the show. He of course winds up on the right side of the law, but not before he steals a cash box and leads the cops on a chase with a car he has stolen. Frankie does another one of his trademark jumps into a convertible without opening the door. There is not a dull minute in the sixty minute film.

Three years after completing his last serial, *The Phantom Empire*, Frankie wound up in a thankless role in the Columbia serial *The Great Adventures of Wild Bill Hickok*. Frankie plays a character named Jerry, an American Indian who pops up occasionally to help out star Bill Elliot before being pushed off a cliff and killed. The serial did nothing for Frankie's career, but it did provide him with a job. As always, his philosophy was, just keep on working.

On April 24, 1939 Frankie paid the required $13 fee to join the American Federation of Radio Artists. He joined as an associate member, one whose gross annual income from radio would be under $2,000 per year. Frankie joined the guild so that he could appear in a radio adaptation of the Warner Bros. film *Angels With Dirty Faces* that was broadcast on The Lux Radio Theater on May 22, 1939. Jimmy Cagney and Pat O'Brien, stars of the film, recreated their roles on the radio drama. Frankie plays one of the young gang members who admires gangster Rocky Sullivan, played by Cagney. Frankie doesn't have much to do, but it does give him a chance to work with Cagney again. The show was not Frankie's sole radio appearance but seems to be the only one to have survived.

The following year Frankie would be immortalized in film history, even though the film going public would never know the name of the voice in this classic film. Walt Disney made animated film history with the release of the first animated feature film entitled *Snow White and the Seven Dwarfs*. His follow up was based on the classic novel by Carlo Corolli entitled *Pinocchio* the story of a wooden puppet that wishes to become a real boy. The tale was popular long before its release as a film.

In the story Pinocchio winds up riding a coach to Pleasure Island, a place where children can supposedly have unsupervised fun all day long, without any responsibilities. With him in the coach is a young boisterous lad named Lampwyck, voiced by Frankie. Once inside the medieval style castle Lampwyck shows Pinocchio the joys of being an unruly kid. These activities include cigar smoking, beer drinking and billiard playing. As the boys go willingly about enjoying their newfound freedom, there is of course a price to pay. Unbeknownst to Pinocchio and Lampwyck, the other boys on the island are slowly turning into donkeys. Once the transformation is complete, they are sold as slaves. Once Lampwyck begins his change, Frankie lets loose with some mournful screams for help. With only five minutes of screen time Frankie and the animators create a truly memorable screen characterization. Pinocchio is voiced by Dick Jones, who worked previously with Frankie on *Little Men* and the serial *The Adventures of Wild Bill Hickok.* They would work together again, almost ten years later on *Sons of New Mexico.*

As was the custom with Walt Disney at the time, he withheld screen credit to the voice actors, so Frankie's name does not appear on the film, which is still highly popular almost seventy years after its initial release. Frankie was proud of the film, even though most people never knew he was the voice of Lampwyck. New generations of children who will never know the name Frankie Darro are still being entertained by him.

Frankie received an intriguing call in the early days of 1941 from John Huston, the well regarded screenwriter who was in preproduction at Warner Bros. Studios on his directorial debut film entitled *The Maltese Falcon.* Humphrey Bogart was cast to play the quintessential private eye Philip Marlowe, and the cast included Frankie's costar from *Red Hot Tires*, Mary Astor. Huston requested Frankie to read for the part of Wilson Cook, the gunsel. After Frankie did the test, Huston seemed very pleased with his reading. The film was to be a major A release, a film that surely would help him get better parts in A films. Unfortunately, Huston's next call to Frankie was a polite, "Thanks, but the part is going to Elisha Cook, Jr." Knowing what an important film it was to be, Frankie was disappointed but his disappointment was tempered when he saw the final film and realized just how effective Cook was in the role.

Watching the film today it's quite easy to picture Frankie in that role too. It could have easily given his career the bump it needed at the time. It did wonders for Cook, who spent the rest of his career playing variations of his character in *The Maltese Falcon*, and doing a very good job of it.

Republic Studios, a B studio with A aspirations, hired Frankie for a solid supporting role for their December 1941 release of *Tuxedo Junction*. The film plays like a Dead End Kids film, with a little music thrown in for good measure. Frankie plays the tough kid who refuses to accept the hospitality of a farm family, played by the popular Weaver Brothers (Leon and Frank) and Elviry, played by their sister June Weaver.

The film has the typical quick Republic pacing and features such popular B stars as Clayton Moore, Lorna Gray and Billy Benedict. It also features a catching title tune, and Frankie is given a love interest, played by Sally Payne. They both play off each other so well, in the dramatic as well as comedy scenes, that it's a shame they never were paired up in subsequent films.

As the parts in major films began to dry out, Frankie realized that he had had his shot at A movie stardom. He became aware that all he was wanted for was to play jockey roles. Apparently even some of Frankie's fans were hoping for more substantial parts for him, as confirmed by a letter to the editor of a movie fan magazine at the time, where a fan queried why Frankie wasn't given better roles. The writer stated that Frankie was more talented than Mickey Rooney, Rooney being one of the most popular stars in Hollywood at the time. The major studios failed to use Frankie as effectively as they might, but there was one studio that did realize Frankie's potential as an actor and a star, one studio that would even give him the coveted above the title billing. While its films were mostly dismissed at the time, this studio certainly entertained its audiences, and many of its films are still thoroughly enjoyable today.

Perhaps the studio's biggest accolade was in 1959, long after it had changed names to hide its B movie past, French director Jean-Luc Goddard dedicated his masterpiece *Breathless* to that studio. The studio was Monogram Pictures Corporation.

CHAPTER 8
LAST STOP MONOGRAM

In 1935 B movie studio Monogram Pictures Corporation and Nat Levine's equally B studio Mascot Pictures merged with Herbert J. Yates's Consolidated Film Industries to form Republic Pictures Corporation, Inc. It took Monogram founder W. Ray Johnson just one year to realize that the merger had been a mistake. Fortunately for Johnson he had sold the business but not the name. So, along with former executive director Trem Carr he split from Republic and revived the name. Monogram was back in the movie business again. Initially the company had leased studio space from Universal Pictures, but before long they settled into their permanent location in East Hollywood at Sunset Boulevard and Hoover.

Monogram specialized in series pictures and westerns. Among its best known series were the Charlie Chan films, (originally produced by 20th Century Fox) and the East Side Kids (later renamed The Bowery Boys) which featured the remnants of the Dead End Kids. Its westerns featured the like of Buck Jones and Tim McCoy. The joke around Hollywood was that if you worked at Monogram your career was either on its way up (if you were new to the business) or on its way down (if you were a veteran). Actor Stanley Clements, featured in many East Side Kids and Bowery Boys movies, once commented that "if you were employed at Monogram, even the out of work actors at Schawbs Drug Store felt sorry for you."

Frankie had been unable to secure a contract with the major studios, so he was delighted when Monogram contacted him and offered him a non-exclusive contract. It was the best of both worlds for Frankie. He had a guarantee of employment, and he was able to work at any other studio, as long as it would not interfere with the production of one of his Monogram films. Frankie would make a total of eleven films for Monogram before the outbreak of World War II. While none are considered classics in the common use of the term, they are all highly entertaining and still enjoyable when viewed today. A big bonus for Frankie was that for the first time in his career he would obtain sole above the title billing. Star billing had always eluded Frankie at the majors, even at Mascot and Conn, but at Monogram Frankie was finally a star.

Monogram employed quick shooting schedules, a seven to ten day shoot was the norm, but even three to four day shoots were not unheard of. Being a veteran of the B style of film making, Frankie was used to this type of hectic work pace, and it suited him just fine. First up for Frankie at Monogram was a sixty minute film entitled *Wanted by the Police*. Released in September 1938, Frankie plays Danny, a young man who becomes the sole support of his mother after his sister marries a policeman. In order to bring in some much needed cash, he gets a job at a local auto garage. Frankie is implicated in an auto theft racket, but he eventually leads the cops to the mob that operates the racket, but not before a rousing car chase that leads to a fiery crash. The film gathered mostly positive reviews, with Frankie consistently singled out for praise. *The New York Times* made mention in its review that Frankie looked no older than he did when he played Little Bill the war orphan in *Roaring Rails* in 1924, additionally commenting, "We feel sure Twentieth Century Fox would appreciate it if Frankie would sell Shirley Temple his secret."

Tough Kid-1938.

88

Three months later Monogram released *Tough Kid.* Frankie has one of the most dramatically powerful scenes of his career near the beginning of the film. After he is accused of stealing a radio, a beat cop and the store proprietor follow him to an apartment to retrieve the stolen radio. Frankie opens the door and we see a bedridden young boy listening to the radio in question. Frankie doesn't have the heart to ask for it back. He glares at the store owner and growls, "You take it." His reading of the line is heart breaking. The boy is allowed to keep the radio. By this point in his career Frankie had effectively honed his body movements, which had always been well displayed.

To watch him in his Monogram films is to see an actor moving with all the style and grace of a ballet dancer. Even simple bits of business, like tapping a table when he leaves the room, effectively add to his characterizations. The film is a little heavy on melodrama, but for the time it went over fine. It was just what post depression audiences needed to be reminded of, that their children might be full of spirit and flexing their independence but they basically are good kids inside.

Even though Monogram was always a B studio and didn't aspire to the occasional A film like Republic did, *Tough Kid,* and the other films Frankie made prior to the war always had decent production values. They were certainly better than the Conn films; however unlike the Conn films, they rarely went out on location.

However, while Frankie's film career was doing fine, his personal life was beginning its long slide downwards, his battle with alcohol remaining a constant problem and growing worse as the hectic filming schedules continued. On December 17, 1938 Frankie turned twenty-one. Befitting a successful young actor, he threw himself a party. Frankie loved card games-poker, Blackjack or anything as long as you could wager on it. Most of the evening was spent in a smoky haze, playing cards and drinking with his friends. By mid evening Frankie had drunk himself into a stupor. His former Lawlor classmate, former child actress Peggy Montgomery, once known as Baby Peggy, recalls seeing him looking "white as a sheet." It would be the last time that she would set eyes on her former crush.

Frankie would use alcohol more and more to retreat from the pressures and responsibilities of professional life. To add even more pressures to his life, just a few days after his birthday his father announced that they were broke. Frank Sr. admitted that he lied about putting money aside for Frankie. The nest egg he was to receive upon turning twenty-one was a big fat nothing. Instead of suing his father for mishandling his funds, Frankie shrugged it off. He could have at least tossed his father out on his ear, but he didn't.

Never a warm father, Frank Sr. was incapable of fatherly love toward Frankie. Frankie hung in and would keep supporting his old man as best he could, but the pressures kept mounting. Now the bottle was rarely far away. As if it was some sort of dark consolation prize, the court ruled on Frankie's birthday that he was now finally in charge of his own bank account and income. At least he was still a popular in demand actor, and as such the money was still rolling in.

In July 1939 Monogram released *Boy's Reformatory*. In this film Frankie was back working with his buddy Frank Coughlin, Jr. for the first time since *Charlie Chan at the Race Track*. The film is another family melodrama with Frankie cast as the good stepson taking the blame for a crime committed by his stepbrother, the aforementioned Coughlin, Jr. Frankie takes the rap to save his stepmother the heartbreak of learning the truth about her no good son. Frankie eventually breaks out of reform school and leads the cops to the head of the crime syndicate.

Coughlin, Jr. is a little weak in the role. His voice is too high pitched for a character who's supposedly a hated rat, but Frankie shines again, especially in the scenes with his step mother. Perhaps due to the fact that Frankie never had a stable relationship with his mother or father, he seems to really bare his soul when acting with any of his movie parents. His longing for such relationship is not far from the surface.

Seventeen days after the release of *Boy's Reformatory* Frankie announced his engagement to Aloha Wray, a wannabe actress he had first met while attending Lawlor's Professional School back in 1931. With his increasing use of alcohol and his inability to remain faithful to one woman, it wasn't the best decision for either one to make. After the realization that his nest egg was non existent, Frankie continued his out of control spending. Financial planning for the future was not even a question. "I made it, and I spent it." he was fond of saying in later years. He wrangled Aloha a bit part in his next movie, but it would be one of only three films in which she would ever appear. The couple was married on Sunday afternoon July 23, 1939 by Reverend Glenn D. Puder at the Immanuel Presbyterian Church in Glendale. Their honeymoon was a trip by car to Humbolt County in Northern California. On their return he and Aloha lived in his house in Beverly Hills.

Frankie and Aloha Wray file a notice of intention to wed-July 18, 1939.

Unbeknownst to Monogram of anyone else at the time, Frankie's next movie would make motion picture history. Unfortunately most film buffs don't realize the historical significance of *Irish Luck*. The film was released in August 1939. For the first time in a Monogram film Frankie was given a screen partner. That partner was none other than black comic actor Mantan Moreland. Moreland was born on September 4, 1901 in Monroe, Louisiana. At the age of twelve he ran away from home, joined the circus and later became a mainstay on the vaudeville circuit. The years on the road honed his comic timing to perfection. He was able to get laughs from just a simple expression or gesture and was often the best thing in a film, even though his parts were for the most part supporting ones. *Irish Luck* was his second film for Monogram, his first being a Tex Ritter western, *Riders of the Frontier*, released earlier the same month. Moreland was put under contract by Monogram and would enliven dozens of their programmers, from his running part as the chauffeur in the Charlie Chan films to his hilarious work in *King of the Zombies*. Moreland would receive his fair share of criticism for the portrayals over the years. I'll leave his non-Darro films for others to criticize, but for the most part in the Darro films, he's not only extremely funny but, along with Frankie, the smartest in the cast. Moreland was given subservient roles to play, but he never played them subserviently. It was Frankie's idea to cast Moreland in his films. Frankie had seen him perform on the stage in Los Angeles and was impressed by his sharp wit and timing. Moreland liked the idea of the pairing but had to make one concession to the times. To appease theater owners in the southern states, Moreland would have to refer to Frankie as Mr. Frankie or, in the case of *Irish Luck*, Mr. Buzzy. They would not put up with black actors being too familiar with their white costars. This concession does not detract from the camaraderie between the two actors.

Monogram must receive the credit for the first pairing of a white and black actor as a team, something the major studios would never dare touch at the time. They would also cast Asian actor Keye Luke in the later Darro films, playing non-stereotypical roles. In *Irish Luck* Mantan receives only seventh billing and never really teams with Frankie until the finale. They do not share the same camaraderie they would share later in the series, and Moreland's frightened persona would be toned down in subsequent films.

In *Irish Luck* Frankie portrays a self-styled amateur detective who is trying to solve a murder at the hotel where he is employed. Actor Grant Withers, Frankie's co-star from *Boy's Reformatory*, makes his producing debut with this film. He would produce two other films in the series before producer Lindsley Parsons took over that chore. Unfortunately, the film suffers from claustrophobia, not an uncommon malady with B films. It takes place almost entirely in the interior of a hotel set. *Variety* liked the film, however, and singled out Frankie, character actor James Flavin and cameraman Harry Newman for their fine work. The film was written by author and theater critic Mary McCarthy who would later write the popular novel "The Group". She was also the sister of cult actor Kevin McCarthy. McCarthy based her screenplay on a novel entitled "Death Hops the Bells." The poorest aspect of the movie is its lack of musical score. What score there is has been culled from library cues, and even then it is used infrequently. Without the music, some scenes lack the punch that they would have had otherwise. The scores would be much improved in the later entries.

Next up at Monogram was the January 30, 1940 release of *Chasing Trouble*. The film was released in just over four weeks after filming was completed.

Frankie and Mantan, finally a real team this time, are delivery drivers for a florist. They get mixed up with a gang of crooks and are entangled in a murder mystery. Frankie tries to solve the murder using his hobby of graphology. Mantan is kicked up to third billing in this entry. *Variety* complained about the weak script, by Mary McCarthy again, but as with most of their Monogram entries, this film really moves. Running a scant sixty-four minutes the pace is lightening quick.

Chasing trouble was also what Frankie and Mantan were doing after hours as well. The two hit if off immediately after their first film and became close friends after working hours. After a long day of shooting Frankie and Mantan would often go out to a bar and have a couple of drinks to unwind. On one such occasion they picked out what they thought would be a quiet bar in Hollywood, not far from the studio. While sitting at the bar sipping their drinks and minding their own business, a small fight broke out. They tried to ignore it, but in a flash the whole place erupted in a brawl. Frankie decided to join in the melee, so he jumped up on the bar and started to kick the various fighters with his feet. They left as quickly as they could, but not before Frankie got some solid kicks and punches in. Mantan was very impressed with Frankie's agility as a fighter.   With Mantan or someone else from the studio or frequently alone, Frankie would almost always stop off at a bar after a day's work. Going home to Aloha was usually not in his plans.

Six months later came the release of *On the Spot*. Frankie and Mantan are a soda jerk and porter, this time around, respectively and both are part time amateur detectives. They know too much about a murder and must solve the killing before they become the next victims. Frankie's love interest in the film is played by ex-Our Gang member Mary Kornman. After the film wrapped, she quit the movie business. Monogram could do that to an actor. Also in the cast is Leroy Mason (his frequent costar during his days with Conn), playing a gangster by the name of Smiling Bill.

In Michael H. Price and George E. Turner's excellent book "Forgotten Horrors 2", the authors suggest that in *On the Spot* Frankie is "almost a generic template for Michael J. Fox." This fact could apply to all his prewar Monogram films.

Six months later on August 12, 1940 *Laughing at Danger* was released.   The setting is a beauty parlor whose operator is in the blackmail racket. He records gossip from his wealthy clientele for use in his racket, and of course a couple of murders are woven into the plot. Frankie is a pageboy for the salon, and along with Mantan they crack the case before the police do. *Variety* enjoyed the film and stated that Moreland "virtually steals" the movie. Monogram realized that they had a hit formula on their hands and mounted an extensive publicity campaign to inform theater owners just how good the series was.

Less than a month later, on September 9, Monogram released *Up in the Air*, the highlight of the series. Frankie and Mantan team up to solve yet another murder, this one at the radio station where they are employed. There never was a lack of murders in Monogram movies!

Frankie and Mantan Moreland in *Up in the Air*-1940.

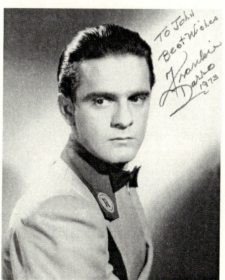

Up in the Air-1940.

The budget seems to have increased over previous entries. Even *Variety* noted that the "production itself is relatively lavish and noteworthy." One review went so far as to call the film "one of the most entertaining pictures to come out of Monogram studio since its reorganization," not bad for a little studio than often had its films dismissed by the trades and ignored by the major papers. Frankie's energy level, always in high gear during the series, is cranked up even higher in *On the Air.* He seems to run in and out of every scene he's in. He shows up at the beginning of the movie dressed in a suit and fedora, passing himself off as an executive at the radio station. He certainly looks the part, but it's only a ruse as he's actually a page. Frankie is joined by janitor Mantan as they try to solve the murder of a prima dona radio star played by Lorna Gray. When reminiscing about her working with Frankie, Ms. Gray (who changed her name to Adrian Booth) let out a sigh and said, "Frankie, he was such a dear!" Along the way they perform a vaudeville routine of their own proposed radio show. The routine was one that Mantan had honed to perfection on the stage. Called "Indefinite Talk", one person would start a sentence and the other would fill in the rest of the sentence. The routine would continue without anyone ever completing a full sentence, but both actors would know exactly what each one was talking about. It's a little disconcerting to see it played out with Frankie in black face, but this was considered humorous in the 1940's and not meant as a jab to anyone's heritage. Perhaps the funniest aspect of the routine as played by Frankie and Mantan is that Frankie tells Mantan there is no need for him to do it in dialect because he will be playing the straight man! Mantan loved working with Frankie but he was not too happy with his performance on the Indefinite Talk routine. He thought Frankie was too quick with his delivery, and Mantan even mentions this during the film. When they wrap up their rehearsal he states "you've got to talk slower if you want me to keep up with you." We are also treated to a couple of songs and a car chase. It all adds up to sixty-one minutes of lighting fast fun. Monogram must have liked the film too, for in 1945 they remade it as *There Goes Kelly* with Jackie Moran and Sidney Miller in the Frankie and Mantan roles respectively.

Up in the Air, now in public domain, was released on DVD by Alpha Video in 2003. The front cover of the package featured a nice color tinted picture of Frankie, Mantan and costar Marjorie Reynolds. Alpha Video gave Mantan above the title billing with no mention of Frankie! With the rise of Mantan's stature as a cult figure in recent years, it is an understandable move. However, it would have been nice if they had been finally billed as the team they really were.

Frankie and Mantan Moreland in *You're Out of Luck*-1941.

In January 1941 came the release of *You're Out of Luck*. Mantan finally receives well deserved second billing for this one. Frankie and Mantan are working at a hotel this time, Frankie as the elevator operator and Mantan as a porter. Working at entry level jobs was their lot in life at Monogram, and once again they are out to solve another couple of murders. One of the highlights of the film is when Mantan is at the police station looking through a book of mug shots trying to identify a suspect in a murder he witnessed. Thumbing through the book he spots various relatives and finally runs across a photo of himself and exclaims in that indignant way he has mastered, "I was not stealing that hog, I was only teaching him how to run!" Mantan's value to the series cannot be overstated. His comic timing is second to none, and he can milk a laugh out of just about any line of dialogue. It's a joy to watch Frankie and Mantan work together. Even a casual viewer realizes that they are really enjoying themselves up on the screen. At one point in the film Frankie gives an out of character laugh after Mantan says his line, and the look on Frankie's face says, "Hey, this guy is really funny!" In its less than positive review of the film, *The Hollywood Reporter* took note of Mantan's role by stating, "Mantan Moreland is outstanding and proves once again he merits a major break." The review in *The Edwardsville Intelligencer* was even more complimentary toward Moreland, stating, "The film is almost completely stolen by Mantan Moreland," and continuing, "…it's surprising that other producers have not taken advantage of the man's outstanding ability."

On June 11, 1941, six months following the release of *You're Out of Luck*, Monogram released the series' penultimate entry entitled *The Gang's All Here*. As the film opens Frankie and Mantan are living out in the sticks like a couple of hobos. Realizing that they are going to need to eat soon, Frankie notices a want ad in a newspaper for long haul truck drivers. They apply for the job, little knowing that the owner of the company is in cahoots with a crooked insurance agent and is actually collecting money for staging accidents with his own trucks. Frankie and Mantan bust the scam with the help of Keye Luke, who plays an undercover insurance investigator. No other studio at the time would cast an Asian actor in such a prominent non-stereotypical role. Jackie Moran and Marcia Mae Jones were also in the cast. They had their own series at Monogram until the previous year. Jones had once had a promising career at MGM. She thoroughly enjoyed working with Frankie and respected his talent, but unlike Frankie she did not enjoy the experience. When asked in 2006 about Monogram, she stated flatly, "I hated it!" She also added that "Frankie would blow the other actors off the screen." The film is another fine entry but does not really need the sub plot filled with Moran and Jones.

On July 18, 1941 Frankie and Aloha announced their separation. Their divorce followed shortly afterwards. Aloha's life after Frankie is unknown, except for the fact that she committed suicide in 1968.

Monogram changed the formula a bit for the final entry in the series. While in production the film was entitled *Sweet Sixteen*, a curious title for a movie eventually titled *Let's Go Collegiate* and was released on September 12, 1941. The most unfortunate change effected by the producer, Lindsley Parsons, is that Mantan is reduced to playing a chauffeur. He's no longer in league with Frankie as usual, but he's the driver for Frankie and some of his college buddies. He keeps his screen name Jeff, but it's a subservient role and he is no longer on equal footing with Frankie. The plot has Frankie and his fraternity brothers trying to pass off a truck driver they pulled off the street as being a famous collegiate athlete. They need the strong as an ox truck driver to help them with an upcoming boat race.

The film plays more like one of the post war Teen Ager series entries. It includes a lot of good swing music, and even Mantan gets a chance to sing! Frankie does a funny reaction take when after asking a girl to dance she replies, "You're too short!" It's a great take, and he takes the slam in stride. The film moves at a rapid pace but it's unfortunate that the series couldn't have concluded with Frankie and Mantan together as a team.

Following the release of *Let's Go Collegiate*, Frankie invited Mantan to accompany him to a party in the Hollywood Hills. It was touted to be a big wild party, the kind Hollywood does best. Mantan couldn't resist the invitation. On the night of the party Frankie drove his shiny roadster through the winding hills and located the home where the party was being held. They walked up the steep path to the front door and rang the bell. The butler opened the door and escorted them to the cloakroom. They were both dressed to the nines, but instead of checking in their coats, they were requested to check in all their clothing! Mantan asked Frankie just what kind of party this was. Frankie didn't know, so he pulled back the curtain that led to the ballroom to have a peek. The orchestra was blaring out its music and the guests were crowded on the dance floor. Everyone including the orchestra was naked! Mantan spotted Little Johnny, the Philip Morris spokes midget dancing with a tall blond. As he was only 3'7", he only came up to her crotch, which for Johnny was probably okay. The two men loved a good party but neither wanted to strip down, so they left and went to a local bar for a drink.

Frankie and Mantan never would appear in another film together, but they did become lifelong friends due to the series. It's unfortunate that in the annals of motion picture history the historic teaming of Frankie and Mantan is largely forgotten. The authors of "Forgotten Horrors 2" make a good case for giving the series its due, but except for them, film scholars have forgotten these little gems.

Forty years before Eddie Murphy teamed with Nick Nolte on the silver screen and thirty years before Bill Cosby teamed with Robert Culp on television, Frankie and Mantan solved murders and made the audience laugh in the process. They made motion picture history, in their partnering even if few realize it.

Less than three months after the release of *Let's Go Collegiate*, Pearl Harbor was bombed by the Japanese, and Uncle Sam was about to call Frankie for duty to his country.

CHAPTER 9
IN THE NAVY

By early 1941, life was treating Frankie very well indeed. Although he didn't make the break into substantial roles in A films as he had hoped for, he was a star at Monogram, and his films were loved by the public. Some were even well reviewed, and even the ones that were given lousy reviews usually singled out Frankie for praise. His heavy drinking continued unabated, but at the age of twenty-four, he could certainly handle all night drinking binges and then show up on the set at 8 a.m. looking clear-eyed and ready for a full day's shoot. As life often does, it took an abrupt turn for Frankie, as it did for all Americans on December 7, 1941. The draft had been reinstated the previous year on a limited basis, but following the United States' entry into the war all, able bodied men between the ages of 18-45 knew it was just a matter of time before Uncle Sam came calling. Frankie knew his days as a civilian were numbered so he beat the draft board to the punch by joining the Navy. He had always loved the ocean. Any time a friend offered to take him out on a boat or better yet, a trip to Catalina, Frankie would always accept the invitation.

With his induction date still a few months away, Frankie used the time to take care of personal business and then decided to take a small part in a film away from his home studio Monogram. Monogram assured Frankie that his contract would be continued upon his return after the war. Frankie took a one day job over at Universal with a part in a serial entitled, *Junior G-Men of the Air.* The twelve chapter serial featured the Dead End Kids (or at least what was left of them by 1942). Leo Gorcey and Bobby Jordan had split from the group to form the East Side Kids over at Frankie's home studio at Monogram. The serial was a follow up to the earlier *Junior G-Men*, released in August 1940.

Junior G-Men of the Air was the best serial of the three that the Dead End Kids made at Universal. It turned out to be an action packed chapter play that could almost stand in the same league as the classics produced Republic at the time. Unfortunately, Frankie has almost nothing to do in the serial. Playing a character named Bob, he is seen briefly at the G-Men headquarters in chapter one, and then he returns in chapter four to check fingerprints on a gun. He returns in chapter ten for one line of dialogue as he hands a piece of paper to costar Frank Albertson. His role could almost have been played by an extra, but it did give Frankie another paycheck before the inevitable pay cut that comes with being in the service.

In April 1942 at the age of twenty-four, Frankie checked into Navy boot camp in San Diego, California. After basic training he went through Hospital Corps School at the San Diego Naval Training Station and graduated as a Pharmacist's Mate, eventually obtaining the rank of First Class. Later when asked why he chose the Hospital Corps, he laughed and replied, "I didn't, the Navy chose it for me."

Just prior to being shipped overseas Frankie decided to try his luck at marriage once again. He had been dating twenty-two year old Betty Marie Morrow. She was a native of Tulsa, Oklahoma and worked as a cashier and part time cocktail waitress. She (like Frankie) had been previously married and was currently living in nearby Long Beach. The ceremony took place on March 16, 1943 at the Long Beach Naval Hospital and was performed by Navy Chaplain Wendell Wheeler. They had a short honeymoon, as Frankie was only weeks away from shipping out.

Once deployed, the newly married Frankie was sent to the South Pacific for an extended tour of duty, taking him to Guam, Australia and eventually many of the smaller islands throughout the area to work in advance base hospitals. His duties included giving booster shots to the ground troops, taking blood samples and helping the doctors by giving the wounded blood or blood plasma during surgery. Frankie would have fit in perfectly in the entertainment branch of the Navy, but he did not regret his more active role in the war.

His stint overseas was not all work. He kept an old black and white photo in his personal collection showing him on an unnamed exotic tropical island, standing next to a young topless native girl who is wearing only a grass skirt. Frankie was wearing his uniform, sailor's cap and a big grin. Paradise indeed!

Frankie in the South Pacific.

On his first tour of duty, Frankie contracted the disease that would plague him on and off for the rest of his life, malaria. Malaria was rampant in the warm climate of the South Pacific, where it was spread by the bite of infected mosquitoes.

The symptoms include fever, shaking, chills, headache, muscle aches and tiredness, and as if these were not enough, nausea, vomiting and diarrhea also can occur. If left untreated, malaria can cause death, as it still does to over one million people per year worldwide. Frankie survived, but the symptoms would reoccur off and on throughout the rest of his life. There is no cure for malaria, only treatment for the symptoms. Frankie's treatment of choice was more alcohol!

Frankie, his wife Betty and Mantan Moreland.

By September 1944 Frankie had attained the rank of Sergeant and was stationed at a large hospital in New Guinea and he was a dispensing pharmacist. During his thirty day leave periods Frankie would lay over in San Francisco, then travel south to Los Angeles to talk shop with his pals who were still at Monogram and finally travel to Long Beach to visit his wife Betty. It was during one of these visits that his wife announced they were expecting their first child in January 1945. Right on time, the Darros became proud parents of a baby girl. Betty wanted the child named Daphne, but when Frankie mentioned that to his buddy Mantan Moreland, Moreland protested, "Not Daphne...Darlene." Frankie agreed the name was better, and with the approval of his wife the baby was named Darlene. Frankie would write to Betty often while he was away. His letters were short and to the point-he loved his wife and missed her and their baby, and he couldn't wait for the end of the war when they could be together and be a family. The problem, of course, was that Frankie had never experienced a normal family life and was ill prepared for one once he was back in Hollywood with Betty and Darlene. By May 18, 1945, Frankie was back from the Pacific and stationed at Long Beach.

The war in Europe had ended on May 8, 1945, and the war in the Pacific would end on September 2 of the same year. Frankie was released from the Navy on Sunday, November 11. The following day in Hollywood, Frankie signed his new contract with Monogram Pictures Corporation.

Now, out of uniform and with a wife and child, it was time for Frankie to get back to work and earn a living for his family.

CHAPTER 10
SAM KATZMAN AND HIS TEENAGERS

After his release from the Navy, Frankie at the age of twenty-nine was back in Hollywood and eager to get back to work. Four years was a long stretch away from the screen. The movies had a whole new roster of stars, fresh new actors who came to prominence while Frankie and other actors were off to war. With cash always in short supply, Frankie had to get back to work fast, and he did, back to the studio he left in 1941, Monogram Pictures Corporation. But more changes than just new faces on the screen were beginning to appear in Hollywood.

The era of Horatio Alger-like stories was over. The war had changed the public's appetite for entertainment. Gritty realism was now front and center. Paranoid "noir" crime dramas were populating the nation's screens. The movies released during the war helped the weary public to forget their problems, at least for an hour of so. Post war audiences were treated with stories featuring characters with seemingly overwhelming problems and with few happy endings. Realism coated with cynicism was the favored entertainment for the dawn of the Atomic Age.

Unbeknownst to him at the time but factual in retrospect, Frankie would never star in another film. Sure, there would be plenty of good roles waiting down the line, but his days of stardom in the B world of movie making were over.

There was another problem. People were staying away from the movie theaters. Motion picture attendance had been at an all time high during the war years. To accommodate swing shift workers some movie theaters would remain open twenty-four hours a day. With the end of the war movie attendance began to decline precipitously. Blame for the decline would be cast in many areas. The returning G.I.'s not wishing to return to their rural homes, would instead flock to the big cities, or better still, to the surrounding burgeoning suburbs. The small rural theaters that catered to the B films would soon close up shop, but the biggest threat to film exhibition was looming on the horizon. It was, of course, television. In 1947 only 14,000 television sets were in existence in the United States. Three years later the number had jumped to four million. Four years later that number had exploded to thirty-two million. One no longer had to leave home for visual entertainment.

Back at Monogram Frankie lucked out with a co-starring role in a new series of features entitled *The Teen Agers.* His luck ended when he learned the name of the new producer, a man Frankie knew of through reputation but had never worked for, a man well known in the B movie world: Sam Katzman. Born in New York City on July 7, 1901, he was affectionately known as Jungle Sam due to his plethora of jungle type movies. He enjoyed the nickname so much that he would often sign his name simply Jungle Sam. Perhaps his more appropriate moniker should have been "Teenage Musical Sam." Katzman produced such genre films as *Twist Around the Clock, Don't Knock the Twist,* and *Let's Twist Again,* among many, many others. He was nothing if not prolific. He would produce the first four of the six *Teen Ager* films that Frankie would appear in, including Frankie's final appearance in a serial.

Taken as a whole, the one aspect that seems to pervade the entire series is they all look pretty cheap. It's been stated that none of Katzman's films ever lost money. A quick look at his threadbare films and it's easy to see why.

Apparently Katzman was rather tight with a buck personally as well. Actor Paul Picerni recalled an incident early in his career. While working on a Katzman production for one day, he was owed a check for one hundred dollars, along with a wardrobe check for the amount of twenty-five dollars. When Paul opened up his pay envelope, he only found a check for one hundred dollars. He marched into Katzman's office and demanded the additional check. Katzman quieted down the upset actor, then opened up his desk drawer which was stuffed full of twenty-five dollar wardrobe checks. "Don't be upset Paul," Katzman stated. "If the actors don't ask for their wardrobe checks, I save them until the end of the year, and then I cash them myself!" This was Frankie's new boss.

Katzman had spent the previous five years producing the *East Side Kids* series, also released by Monogram. When Katzman wouldn't meet series star Leo Gorcey's salary demands, Gorcey and his agent Jan Grippo split from Katzman and formed a partnership to produce *The Bowery Boys* series themselves. Before the war Grippo had also been Frankie's agent. Since losing out on the popular *East Side Kids* series, it was a logical step to produce another series about a group of humorous young people, albeit more mild mannered this time.

A most surprising aspect of the series was that Monogram was able to book most of the films into top of the bill play dates. This enabled them to command higher rentals for the films. It was not unusual to have the *Teen Ager* films playing on the top of the bill in one movie theater while one of Frankie's prewar Monogram films played on the bottom of the bill at a different theater in the same town. Monogram kept Frankie's earlier films in constant re-release.

The first entry in the series was entitled *Junior Prom*. Filming commenced in early November 1945 and was completed on the 20th of the same month. It was released six months later on May 11, 1946. The story was a rather simple one, as all in the series would be. Series star Freddie Stewart is running for student body president of Whitney High School. His rival candidate is Jackie Moran. Moran's father has promised to supply uniforms for the football team if his son is allowed to win the election. Frankie plays Roy Dunn, Moran's campaign manager. Frankie is billed fifth, under Jackie Moran, which must have pained Frankie a bit since Moran played in support of Frankie before the war. Frankie isn't given a lot of screen time, but when he's on, he's in there fighting. At the school dance he attempts to woo high school newspaper editor Betty (played by perky Noel Neill) so that she'll write a positive story about Moran. She soon discovers the ruse and is seen later at home reading a book entitled "The Male Beast" as Frankie arrives to pick her up for the prom.

Frankie and Noel have a nice comedy bit at the school election rally. Frankie is giving a campaign speech in support of Moran while being fed the script by Noel. Noel and Frankie work well together and would play a couple throughout the series with the exception of Frankie's final appearance in the series, *Smart Politics*. When asked in 2005 about working with Frankie, Noel smiled and said wistfully, "Ah Frankie, he was so talented!" However she would not or could not impart any memories.

The film abounds with music, seven songs total. Freddie Stewart is a sort of precursor to Frankie Avalon. Off screen as a singer he was a teenage heartthrob, and in the films it appears that everyone is just waiting for him to break into a song, which he does with great frequency. The highlight of the film is a fight between Noel Neil and her sister (played by former MGM contract player and series regular June Preisser). Noel attempts to rip off the sweater June is wearing. June looks startled, and if the scene would have run a few more minutes, it would have made motion picture history!

The film was well received. *Film Daily* on March 1, 1946 stated, "Excellently directed...launches new Teen-ager series to good start." *Variety* agreed, noting "JUNIOR PROM is a slick chick musical review of, by and for teenagers. It has the stuff to 'send' youngsters in a big way and at the same time should be easy to take for the adult portion of the audience." There was a disparaging comment from *The Hollywood Reporter*, which stated that due to the fact both Jackie Moran and Frankie were screen veterans, it was difficult to accept them as juniors in high school. It would be a common complaint during the run of the series, Frankie was twenty-eight years old when the film was released, and Moran was twenty-three.

The second entry in the series was *Freddie Steps Out*. Filming was completed on March 18, 1946, and the film was released on June 29 of that same year. The story concerns a famous crooner who walks out on his popular radio program and promptly disappears. The crooner happens to be the splitting image of Freddie Stewart, who then spends the rest of the film trying to convince everyone that he is not the famous singer. This is a rather difficult proposition since Stewart plays both roles. Frankie's character is a campus Lothario who in one sequence tries to teach the older but less wise Candy Candito the tricks of his trade. The sub plot features an infant who causes nothing but trouble. Everyone in the movie is convinced that the baby belongs to one of the gang or to the principal. Since this is high school and it's 1946, it all plays out in a rather risqué manner.

Marie Picerni, who worked on the film as a dancer recalls being on the set when producer Sam Katzman came in for a visit. He entered the sound stage at Monogram and made his way to where the young girls were waiting for their dance number. He mingled with them and then began to goose the girls with his walking stick. This was Marie's first film, and her introduction to Hollywood film making techniques.

Variety gave a nod to Frankie this time around, stating in its review that "Frankie Darro is a standout." About the film itself *Variety* mentioned, "*Freddie Steps Out* second in the Teen-ager series, is a tuneful medley of bobby-sock entertainment which should hit the bull's eye for market intended." *The Hollywood Reporter* also liked the film but complained again that the cast was too old for high school. They suggested they should by in college. As with all the films in the series the musical sequences seemed to be dropped in at the whim of the producer, but this entry is one of the best in the series.

A couple of weeks before filming began on the third entry in the series, Katzman brought Frankie over to his serial unit at Columbia Pictures to appear in the fifteen chapter serial, *Chick Carter, Detective*. Katzman recently had taken over the producing chores on all Columbia's serials, a move most fans bemoaned as the quality dropped precipitously. The serials would eventually run from poor to unwatchable. *Chick Carter, Detective* was slightly above the unwatchable category. The serial was originally to be called *Nick Carter, Detective*, based on the long-running series of popular novels and radio show, but the copyright holder refused permission to use the name, thus the last minute change. In the serial Frankie plays a character named the Creeper, a hoodlum working for a bigger hood. Frankie appears in eight of the chapters, without billing. At one point in chapter ten he accidentally runs into a sofa. Retakes were a luxury not afforded many Katzman productions. Frankie doesn't have much to do in the serial, other than just sit or stand around in a few scenes, but it was a payday and for Frankie paydays were getting scarce.

Production on the serial ended on May 9, and it was back to Monogram for Frankie. When the first chapter of *Chick Carter, Detective* was released on July 11, it would be Frankie's final appearance in a serial. Serials only had another decade to survive, before becoming another victim of television.

The next entry in the series began production in early May 1946, with shooting completed on May 29. The film was entitled *High School Hero* and was released on September 7, 1946. Spunky June Preisser is front and center this time. It seems Whitney High has not won a football game in twenty-seven years. The coach is about to call it quits when he spots a player making fantastic touchdown at practice. The player turns out to be none other than June, disguised as Warren Mills' character Lee. Though the ruse is discovered, June tells the team to break into a dance routine during the big game to throw off the opposing team. The routine looks ridiculous on the playing field, but it does win the game for them. Preisser, born in 1921, got her start in such MGM musicals as *Babes in Arms* and *Strike Up the Band*. She was an extremely talented dancer with a winning screen persona who rarely seemed to get the roles she deserved. She is featured as Dodie, in all the *Teen Ager* films, but rarely given the spotlight, except in this entry. The entry was a rather weak one, and it afforded Frankie very little screen time. He has a cute slapstick sequence with Noel Neil where they keep butting their heads together, but that's about it. *Film Daily* in its review on August 21, 1946 stated, "This is the best offering in the *Teen-Ager* series..." But it was *Variety* this time complaining about the age of the cast. It wrote that Frankie and Jackie Moran should be postgraduates by now, and also complained about the commercial plugs in the picture, blatant plugs for products such as Capitol Records and Royal Crown Cola. Forty years later, of course, this would be standard operating procedures for most features.

The next film in the series would finally please the critics who complained that the kids were getting too old for high school. The film *Vacation Days* opens with the gang finally graduating from Whitney High School. Running character Mrs. Hinklefink (played by Belle Mitchell) is a teacher at the school who has inherited a ranch out west. She takes the students along with the Principal to her newly acquired property for a little summer R&R. Once they arrive out west, Freddie Stewart is mistaken for the notorious criminal, Angel Face Harriagton. Frankie gets to save the day in this one and does it by leaping into a nearby parked car and chasing after the crook who had stolen some silver. Although Frankie doesn't have a lot of screen time, as usual, he's clearly in support in the entire series. He is seen to good advantage at the conclusion, and it's always fun to see him trying to put the make on cute Noel Neill, who rebuffs him at every turn. *Vacation Days* completed filming on October 21, 1946 and was released on January 25, 1947. Spade Cooley and Jerry Wald along with their popular bands, add some good musical interludes to the proceedings. It's also refreshing to see the location change from Whitney High to somewhere out west, courtesy of the Monogram Ranch in Newhall, California.

Frankie with Noel Neill and June Preisser in *Sarge Goes to College*-1947.

The series would take on a new twist with the next entry. Sam Katzman would turn over producing chores to Will Jason, a director and songwriter, and would exit the series. He moved over to Columbia to continue with his serial and B films. Jason would produce the remaining entries in the series, write some of the songs and direct the films as well. His first entry is entitled *Sarge Goes to College* and was released on May 17, 1947. The film has a strange almost surreal feel to it. Sarge (played amiable by Alan Hale, Jr.) is sent off to San Juan Junior College to relax and build up his strength while awaiting surgery for an under active thyroid condition. Once at the school he meets up with the *Teen Agers*, who are in the process of putting on a big campus show. The film is very slight in the story department, but is full of music, seven musical numbers in all, featuring such musical greats as Les Paul and Russ Morgan. The musical numbers seem to pop up with no good reason but are fun to watch. Jack McVey performs his hit "Open the Door Richard" and there is a hot jam session with Abe Lyman, Candy Candito, Wingy Manone, Les Paul, Jess Stacy, Joe Vanut and Jerry Wald. It's the highlight of the film, if not the series.

Frankie is billed third this time around. He's back having girlfriend problems with Noel Neill, who breaks up with him, until the finale. He also gets to punch out Freddie Stewart. It's a well staged fight scene, showing that Frankie is still as energetic as always. The film ends rather abruptly with Freddie on the telephone singing a love song to Alan Hale, Jr., who is in his hospital bed recovering from surgery. We never do get to see the big musical show that was in the works for the entire sixty-three minute running time, but the seven musical numbers almost make up for it. Besides, with the slim budgets given to these films, a big musical production number would be about the last thing you would expect to see.

While *The Hollywood Reporter* thanked Will Jason for finally taking the series out of high school, *Variety* slammed the film, stating that it fell flat in both plot and music. While it certainly did fall flat in the plot department for fans of mid 1940's music, it can certainly hold its own.

Donald McBride standing over The Teen Agers. Frankie is second on the left.
*Smart Politics-*1948

The next entry in *The Teen Agers* series entitled *Smart Politics* would be Frankie's final appearance with the *Teen Agers*. The film went into production in early September 1947 and completed filming on September 19. The film was released on January 3, 1948. Originally titled *The Old Grey Mayor*, the opening of the film is homage, or more likely a rip off, of *Our Town*. Once past the opening, the film settles down to concern itself with the *Teen Agers* wanting to open up a youth center in their home town of San Juan, supposedly located between Los Angeles and San Diego. Frankie receives third billing again but changes have been made as he's no longer part of the gang. His character name of Roy Dunne remains intact, but this time he's part of a trio of would be thieves. Perhaps Will Jason thought Frankie had outgrown his usual role. The other two gang members are played by popular recording artists the Cappy Barra Harmonica Boys. Frankie might not be part of the gang any longer, but he does have his best role in the series. He no longer has any interest in Noel Neill, but he does get to beat up Freddie Stewart again! He's also given the majority of the plot exposition dialogue to deliver toward the conclusion of the film and does so superbly. Producer Jason knew who the veteran actor was and knew Frankie could deliver the goods. On the minus side, Candy Candito is more aggravating than humorous this time around, but famed drummer and band leader Gene Krupa shows up at the end of the film to make the whole show worthwhile.

The series would continue with one additional entry, but without Frankie. *Campus Sleuth*, next in the series, was released on April 4, 1948. Stewart Preisser, and Neill would appear together in *Music Man*, released on September 5 of the same year, but it was not part of the official series. The conclusion of the series also saw the conclusion of most of the careers of *The Teen Agers*. Star Freddie Stewart and perky June Preisser would never make another movie. Warren Mills would have a very minor role in one movie before later committing suicide. Only Noel Neill and Frankie would continue in movies.

As a whole, it was not a particularly memorable series, but none of the entries ran over seventy minutes long and it did offer some hot musical numbers, okay comedy, and some good work by Frankie.

CHAPTER 11
THE BOWERY BOYS

With the demise of Frankie's participation in *The Teen Agers* series Monogram promptly put him in additional supporting roles in their popular Bowery Boys series. Frankie's pal Mantan Moreland was still being employed by Monogram, playing the chauffeur in the *Charlie Chan* series. Neither actor was given better roles, and apparently no thought was given to a re-teaming.

Conventional wisdom is to afford the Bowery Boys little or no respect. If mentioned at all these days, it is to dismiss the series as low brow humor that audiences might have enjoyed at the time but were cheap B films that were basically ostracized by critics of the era and are now ignored by the current generation of film buffs, who cling to The Three Stooges as being the height of low brow humor. However, this is only partly factual.

Amazingly, The Bowery Boys series ran from 1946 to 1959, long after most other series films had tossed in the towel, and they encompassed some forty-eight feature films, a prodigious output by anyone's standards, enormously popular at the time of their initial release and even more so when released to television. In his introduction monologue for the Academy Awards ceremony in the early 1950's, comedian Bob Hope joked that when he turns on the television all he sees are old Bowery Boys films.

Many baby boomers had their first introduction to Frankie while watching the four features he made with the Boys during their numerous television airings throughout the 1950's and beyond.

While not individually diverse roles, three were good substantial parts, with one great part thrown in for good measure. For Frankie, whose film career was slowly sinking into oblivion, the series showed he was still capable of shining if given half a chance. The series also provided him with his last four roles at Monogram Studios, the studio with which he had been associated since 1938. The series was not his first experience working with the remnants of The Dead End Kids, of course, he had, appeared in the serial *Junior G-Men of the Air* with the

Dead End Kids/Little Tough Guys in 1942. The Bowery Boys would be the final incarnation of the original Dead End Kids, with only Leo Gorcey, Huntz Hall and Gabriel Dell still hanging around from the original group. Dell would leave the series by the end of 1950. It is perhaps best to look at the films as being the Gorcey and Hall series, since in actuality the Bowery Boys are rarely around. They are usually sent on some mission early on by Gorcey, and then meet up with him and Hall at the conclusion of each film. If they are featured in the bulk of the film, they are afforded little or no dialogue. Gorcey and Hall are the whole show but have undeniable chemistry. They could provoke laugher from any situation and are just as funny today as Abbott and Costello, the celebrated comedy team of the same era.

The films were produced by Jan Grippo, Gorcey's agent, along with Gorcey himself. Monogram released the films until 1953 when Monogram, in an effort to polish its image, changed its name to Allied Artists. After the name change the films became all comedy, a switch from the comedy-dramas of the Monogram years. The films were made quickly. Billy Benedict (who played Whitey in the series) recalled one feature that was completed in just two days! Five to seven days was the norm.

Frankie's first film in the series was completed on November 20, 1947. It was entitled *Angel's Alley* and was released on March 21, 1948. In the film Frankie plays Jimmy (cousin to Leo Gorcey's Slip Mahoney), a small time crook and two time loser who gets mixed up with local crime boss Tony LaCarno, who convinces him to pull off a heist of a local warehouse. Gorcey tries to save his cousin from becoming a three time loser but is himself charged with the crime. Frankie turns over a new leaf when he realizes Gorcey almost went to jail for the crime. Frankie receives sixth billing in this entry, but it's a strong costarring role that belies such low billing.

Frankie's first scene has him locking horns with Gorcey. When Gorcey arrives at his apartment and is greeted by his mother (played by perennial Irish mom Mary Gordon, who was in reality Scottish!), Frankie enters wearing Gorcey's robe and pajamas. Frankie's surly demeanor when questioned about the clothing is a delight. Frankie and Gorcey work well together in the first of many on screen meetings. The film is a little heavy on the dramatics, but all and all it's a fine entry in the series. Huntz Hall lightens the tone at the conclusion of the film when he gets fed up with Gorcey picking on him and states, "This is the last picture I make with you!" Hall would break character on occasion during the run of the series.

Frankie with Leo Gorcey and Mary Gordon in *Angels Alley*-1948.

The *Motion Picture Herald* on January 24, 1948 stated in its review, "The picture is tops for the series." *Angels Alley* was a fine entry indeed, but Frankie's best was still a few pictures away.

On Sunday, May 23, 1948 while Frankie was in production on his next Bowery Boys film, tentatively entitled *High Tension,* he received his only known honor for his long acting career. The cities of Arroyo Grande and Pismo Beach, California held their two day All Star Jamboree with Frankie as the guest star. Upon his arrival he was met by members of the Arroyo Grande Lion's Club, Rotary Club, Businessmen's Association, Women's Club, Civic Club and other groups and was presented with the keys to both cities. During the Jamboree Frankie introduced the candidate for the Fiesta queen, Joan Monk.

Following the two day fiesta it was back to work until his current film wrapped on May 28. The movie's title was changed to *Trouble Makers* in time for its December 10 release. Frankie is fourth billed this time around. For some unknown reason his character's name is Feathers. The film's back story has Frankie and Gabe Dell growing up together in an orphanage. Gabe became a cop, walking the beat in the Bowery, while Frankie became a hood. The Bowery Boys are trying to solve a murder case at a local hotel with the help of their old buddy Gabe. John Ridgely plays the main villain, with Frankie relegated to the supporting villain position. It's interesting to watch Frankie and Ridgely in their scenes together. Even though Ridgely towers over Frankie, when Frankie uses his old finger trick and taps Ridgely on his chest, he does it with such menacing force the he brings Ridgely down to his size. Frankie also puts the classic screen stealer Gorcey in his place. Gorcey, seeing Frankie entering the room, states, "If it isn't number one in the rat race." "Shaddup!" Frankie snaps back. Gorcey takes notice.

Frankie earned a couple of extra dollars on the shoot by doubling for Gorcey in a scene, he's easily spotted hanging from the ledge of the hotel window near the conclusion of the film. The movie has a wonderfully strong supporting cast, including Ridgely (a long time Warner Bros. contract player), Lionel Stander and the always reliable Fritz Feld. The reviews were again positive. The *Hollywood Reporter* stated, *"Trouble Makers* certainly is their most entertaining film to date."* *Variety* also enjoyed the film and reviewed it at its showing at the Grauman's Chinese Theater! So much for Monogram films only playing small rural theaters!

MONOGRAM PICTURES Presents LEO GORCEY and THE BOWERY BOYS in "FIGHTING FOOLS". 19/230
A JAN GRIPPO PRODUCTION with HUNTZ HALL, GABRIEL DELL, FRANKIE DARRO,
LYLE TALBOT and EVELYNN EATON.   Printed in the U. S. A.

Frankie and The Bowery Boys in *Fighting Fools*-1948.

Frankie had his best role of the series in the next entry. The film, initially entitled *Iron Dukes*, began production in late June 1948 and completed production on July 23. Eventually retitled *Fighting Fools*, the film has Frankie playing Johnny Higgins, a down and out ex-boxer who had once killed an opponent in the ring. The Bowery Boys convince Frankie to re-enter the ring in an effort to raise money for a charity. Frankie's first scene shows him in a dingy bar drinking with a local floozy. He looks every bit the dispirited boxer. The tone of the Bowery Boys films tended to shift from one film to another. They could be more comedic or more dramatic depending on the entry, until 1953 when they would shift to pure comedy. This entry relies more on dramatics than usual. Even perpetually confused Sach (played by Huntz Hall) delivers a most uncharacteristic line when he states, "Sister, you don't have a face until you put it on in the morning!" He reads the line straight and then returns to his Sach character. It's startling to see him drop his Sach persona, if only for a second. The dramatics work for the film, which affords Frankie a wonderful role. His character eventually sobers up and returns to the ring to win the big bout. The film was released on April 17, 1949 and earned Frankie a glowing review from the *Hollywood Reporter*, stating in its May 18, 1949 issue, "*Fighting Fools* is in the best tradition of Monogram's Bowery Boys series. To Hollywoodites there is the spectacle of watching Frankie Darro playing a 'kid' fighter at this stage of his life with ease, conviction and a bouncy juvenile air. It happens he has a good role in the show, and Darro is smart enough to make the most of it."

Years later I sat in Frankie's hotel room and showed him the pressbook for *Fighting Fools*. Pressbooks are used by theater owners in preparation for booking a film, and are filled with ads, posters and pre-made newspaper stories about a film and its stars. One story on Frankie mentioned a hobby of wood carving. It stated that for years when starting production on a movie he would begin a wood carving project and by the end of the shoot would invariable have some object completed. "How can they write such lies?" Frankie asked resignedly. "I can't believe that they would write that. I have never carved anything in my life." It's probably a good thing that Frankie never saw the pressbook to one of his Conn films, *Men of Action* which claimed he was an airplane pilot and would take various cast and crew members aloft and do acrobatic loops to acclimatize them to working on the high level Hoover dam!

To pass the time of day on a Bowery Boys set, it was most likely that it would be liquor, not wood, that kept Frankie occupied. Leo Gorcey was a world class drinker himself. Billy Benedict recalled that Gorcey would always have a bottle tucked in his back pocket. Benedict thought Gorcey was actually a better actor after a few belts.

The previous year Huntz Hall had been arrested for marijuana possession and would later be arrested for driving under the influence. If Frankie was drinking between takes, it didn't show in any of his performances.

After completing the filming of *Fighting Fools*, Frankie devised an idea for a stage act with himself and Jackie Moran, his Monogram costar who had lost his contract with the studio two years earlier.

Their premiere engagement was held on Wednesday, August 4, and ran three days. They appeared at The Hawaiian Village at Vermont and 107th Street in Los Angeles. The ad read "They will meet you, seat you, and entertain you. Come on down. Anything can happen and probably will." There is no record of a second engagement. Frankie's final Bowery Boys film started production in mid March 1949, with filming completed on April 8. Entitled *Hold That Baby*, this entry leaned more towards comedy then the previous three films. Frankie plays a character named Bananas, due to his wont for chomping on bananas throughout the course of the film. The story concerns a gang of crooks that is blackmailing the Boys into playing nursemaid for a baby who's just about to inherit a fortune. Frankie plays one of the hoods doing the blackmailing. He looks sharp in his fedora and suit. He has a way of cocking his head in an insolent manner, as if to say, "Don't screw with me." Frankie doesn't have a large role, but it certainly is an interesting character, and Frankie does the most with it.

Frankie with Huntz Hall in *Hold That Baby*-1949.

The film was released on June 26, 1949. In its review of the film on July 29, the *Hollywood Reporter* mentioned, "Frankie Darro's youthful heavy is done expertly." *Hold That Baby* would be not only his final Bowery Boys film, but also his final film at Monogram, his studio home for the past eleven years. When I asked Frankie why he didn't make more films with the Bowery Boys, he simply said, "They wouldn't meet my salary demands. They wanted to use me again; they just didn't want to pay me." Since his personal finances were at a very low point at the time and few other offers were coming in, this doesn't really answer the question, but for whatever reason his tenure at Monogram was over.

The Bowery Boys films still hold up today, providing laughs and entertainment years after their initial release. They also provided Frankie with four substantial roles for his rapidly disintegrating career.

CHAPTER 12
THE RETURN OF WILD BILL

Unlike Frankie's prewar career when he was able to bounce back and forth between A and B film work, life was quite different during his post war period at Monogram. During his three years at Monogram following the war, Frankie was only able to secure roles in two outside films, both of which had him playing jockeys again.

So stated before, Frankie's contract with Monogram was non exclusive, as it had been before the war, and it allowed him to appear in films at other studios. Unlike his prewar career he was unable to find much work at other studios. He would comment in later years that he was always knocking on doors, looking for roles, but the roles were becoming more and more scarce. Frankie, of course, was not the only one having a tough time in the post war film world. Frank Borzage, who had directed Frankie in *No Greater Glory* and *Stranded* back in the mid 1930's, and was once hailed as one of the great directors working in Hollywood, he was now reduced to making films for Republic Pictures. To its credit, Republic saw the writing on the wall for B films and was at least trying to at least get a foothold in the A film market place. Borzage was in production on a horserace film in the spring of 1947 and hired Frankie to play a jockey named Frankie Daniels. The film is entitled *That's My Man* and stars Don Ameche, himself taking a step down from his Twentieth Century Fox days. The plot has Ameche raising a colt named Gallant Man, but his personal life collapses around him due to gambling and drinking. He retires the horse, only to find out that his wife has entered the horse in the Hollywood Gold Cup. The horse wins, and Ameche finds his life turned around. Frankie is billed ninth and plays the jockey who rides Gallant Man across the finish line. The horseracing scenes are taut and exciting. Frankie does all his own riding, and there is little use of rear projection scenes which mar so many racetrack films. Called "lavish but over long" by *Variety*, the film was released on June 1, 1947.

Popular gossip columnist Jimmy Fidler reported on June 6, 1947 that Frankie had punched out his old pal Mickey Rooney while shooting a boxing sequence for the film *Kid McCoy*. Fidler stated at the time, Frankie "…got plenty irked by Mickey's tactics the other day and kayo'd him with a meant-for-business haymaker right to the button." It must have been serious as Frankie is not in the finished film.

The following year Republic hired Frankie for yet another horseracing drama. The film was entitled *Heart of Virginia* and was released on April 10, 1948. Frankie was billed third, below B film stalwart Robert Lowery and Janet Martin.

While offering nothing new in content, the film has the typically good Republic production look and features a wild fight between Frankie and sometime Bowery Boy Bennie Bartlett. Frankie's character suffers from a fear complex due to the death of a jockey that he feels responsible for. The film turns ugly briefly when Frankie is beaten repeatedly with a leather strap by a horse owner (played by Paul Hurst). After the beating, for which Frankie never receives as much as a small apology, it is never mentioned again, and both characters are friends at the finale. Frankie's character is also suffering from an unrequited love for Martin. Lowery winds up with the girl, but Frankie realizes that his true love is simply being a jockey.

Frankie received another complimentary review in *Variety*, "Darro…reads his jockey role capably even offsetting stereotyped dialogue." Frankie was injured during the filming in December 1947 when he was thrown by a horse and wound up in the hospital. His knee was injured, and he had to undergo an operation to repair the damage.

With film work becoming more and more difficult to come by late in 1949, Frankie did something that he had never before considered. He found employment outside the entertainment business. He found a job at Todd's, a clothing store at the corner of First and Locust in Long Beach. His job consisted of selling men's suits. When some of his fans found out about the job, they would come to the store just to gawk at the fading star. He stated that one young girl asked for his tie as a souvenir. When he told her he had to wear it for the job, she responded, "Okay, then give me your shirt!" "Some of them just stand and look at me," he said at the time. "They don't say anything... just stare. That makes me nervous."

To save face Frankie told a local newspaper that he was working at the store just to learn the trade and eventually would open his own store. Generously, his employer let him off work to take the few assignments that did come his way.

On January 29, 1949 Frankie was the master of ceremonies at a March of Dimes function in Long Beach. It wasn't a movie, but it did keep his name in the news, at least for a day. His next film assignment would be from an old friend who was having career problems of his own. Frank Capra, perhaps the greatest of the populist directors in prewar Hollywood, found himself unable to return to his prewar stature. By 1949 he was a Paramount contract director, unable to get any of his pet projects off the ground. The one project Paramount finally green lighted was a remake of his own *Broadway Bill*.

In order to get the film made quickly and cheaply, Capra used stock footage from the original, along with eight members of the original cast so he could match up old and new footage.

Frankie with Clarence Muse and Bing Crosby in Frank Capra's *Riding High*-1950.

Entitled *Riding High*, the new film starred Bing Crosby. Capra had Crosby sing a few unmemorable songs and turned it into a quasi-musical. Since Frankie had been in the original version, Capra hired Frankie to repeat his same role in the remake. Capra doesn't play up the fact that Frankie's jockey is crooked this time around, thus reducing the effectiveness of Frankie's role.

Production began on March 14, 1949 and ran through mid May. Capra took the production company back to Tanforan Park in South San Francisco where the original film had been shot. Frankie always enjoyed his trips to the Bay Area and, this trip would be a special treat for him. Since childhood Frankie had been a fan of the comedy team of Stan Laurel and Oliver Hardy. For this remake Capra hired Hardy for an un-billed cameo. After a long day of filming Frankie and Oliver Hardy traveled over to San Francisco for a night on the town. It was a great experience for Frankie to be able to pal around with his boyhood idol. After dinner the two walked around the city checking out various bars and nightclubs. "Man, he could put away the beer," Frankie would relate with a smile many years later.

When the film was released on April 12, 1950, no one's career benefited. At one preview the audience hooted at the screen, feeling cheated at all the stock footage. Capra re-cut some of the film but it didn't help. Capra had the audacity to open the film with an entire sequence lifted from the original film. It was obvious to anyone that the footage is antiquated, but at least it was a payday for Frankie and paydays were scarce. It was touted as a class A production, and though the role is not a large one, Frankie is in good form. By now whether playing a good jockey or a bad one, Frankie had that role down pat.

Another friend from the past stepped up to give Frankie his next role. Gene Autry had seen his career rise rapidly since his first starring role in the serial *The Phantom Empire*. Along with his producing partner Armand Schaffer, Autry had been cranking out B oaters on a regular basis for years. First releasing through Republic Pictures and then Columbia Pictures. On June 15, 1949 they began production on *Sons of New Mexico*. Filming would be completed two weeks later on

June 29. Frankie, looking fit and healthy, is billed fifth and plays Dick Johnson, a former jockey hired by the character played by Dick Jones to train horses at Jones' ranch. This would be the third time Frankie and Jones would work together. Jones said he enjoyed seeing Frankie again and was impressed with his ability to keep everyone on the set loose with jokes and his winning smile.

Frankie is a heavy this time. He goes so far as to hit Autry over the head with a six shooter. Frankie receives his comeuppance later in the film in a gruesome scene near the conclusion when Robert Armstrong smashes a rifle into Frankie's head, killing him. The film contains some unnecessary padding at a military school, but all and all it's a good B western with a stronger than usual supporting cast. Unfortunately B westerns along with B films in general were seeing their days numbered, Autry would continue making westerns for another three years before switching to television exclusively. In 1987 Autry hosted a cable television program entitled Melody Ranch Theater. He reminisced with his frequent costar Pat Buttram on the making of *Sons of New Mexico*. Commenting on Frankie, Autry said, "He could do everything. He really was a fine little actor." Then he added, "...he gave me a lot of trouble. I think we had a lot of trouble with Frankie on that..." Neither commented on the exact nature of the trouble, but you can be sure it had something to do with alcohol. The chat is included on the DVD release of the film.

Early in 1950 Frankie was hired for another western over at Universal. The film was *Wyoming Mail*, a strictly routine film. Frankie was billed eleventh and has no dialogue. His eye is made up to look deformed, and with a beard added he really looks pretty menacing. Due to his eye makeup the cast and crew didn't want to have him at their lunch table. Frankie took the snub in stride and ate by himself.

In August 1950, popular Hollywood columnist Army Archerd asked Frankie to comment on the continuing flood of parents who bring their children to Hollywood in search of stardom. Frankie responded, "So if your little darling has terrific talent, let him develop it in a local theater and bide his time. Don't bring him here because it's 100 to 1 that he'll never get a chance to use it." Archerd certainly asked the right person.

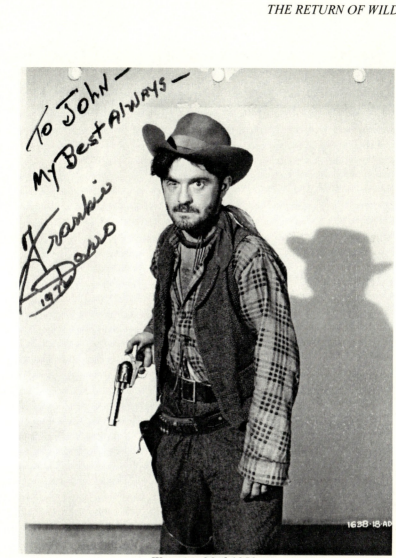

Wyoming Mail-1950.

With little work coming his way, Frankie would hit the bottle more and more frequently. Fortunately for him but unfortunately for his health and career, bars lined the streets of Hollywood at the time. Almost everyone knew his name, and he knew all the bartenders' names. It made the time pass, and he didn't have to think of the money and career problems facing him. When he was drunk, it just didn't matter anymore.

A person out of his past was responsible for his next few assignments. William Wellman was working over at MGM and was able to get Frankie a few parts at the once great, but now struggling, studio. Frankie would thank Wild Bill publicly for his kind gesture. Seventeen years after starring in *Wild Boys of the Road* for Wellman, Frankie has only a three second silent bit part in his third film for the director, the 1950 *The Next Voice You Hear*. In a silent montage Frankie is seen shaking his head "No" in response to James Whitmore asking various people if they had seen his missing son. It was Frankie's briefest screen appearance to date, but at least it was a payday. The same year he also appeared in *A Life of Her Own*, again at MGM. Frankie plays a bellhop in the film starring Lana Turner and directed by George Cukor.

Frankie and Peggy Stewart in *The Pride of the Maryland*-1951.

Frankie received his final shot at star billing with the January 20, 1951 release of *Pride of the Maryland*. Frankie was billed third, after Stanley Clements and Peggy Stewart, but on the poster all three are billed above the title. The Republic release has Frankie and Clements as rival jockeys, with Peggy Stewart caught in the middle. Stewart is married to Frankie, but Clements is an old flame. Even though Frankie plays a jockey again, it's a more well rounded role. He is given a wife and a child, and he plays the part well. Unfortunately, his character dies fifteen minutes into the sixty minute movie, and most viewers probably spent the next forty-five minutes wishing that Frankie was still around. It was also bittersweet to realize his career would take another step down in terms of quality of roles and quantity of screen time.

Later the same year Wellman hired Frankie for his film *Across the Wide Missouri*, a film Wellman did not want to make. He had had trouble with the star Clark Gable years earlier on *Call of the Wild* and had vowed never to work with him again. However MGM allowed Wellman to take his family on location, and he turned the shoot into a working vacation. Frankie has a small un-credited part as one in a group of mountain men who fight Gable and costar John Hodiak. During the fight sequence Frankie jumps on Gable's back and starts punching him. Gable moves over to a lake and promptly tosses Frankie in. During down time on location the company held a ping pong tournament. Day by day more and more contestants were eliminated until the finals were played between Frankie and a French production person who fancied himself a ping pong champ. The cast and crew rooted for Frankie, but his opponent won out in the end, much to the consternation of cast and crew.

Once the film was completed, MGM took the film and re-cut it without Wellman's input. The revised version made so little sense that narration was put in so that viewers could follow the story.

Back in Hollywood in November 1951, Frankie's wife Betty finally threw in the towel, and filed for divorce. They had separated at least twice before, and on one previous occasion Betty had filed for divorce. Her complaints were drinking and money. "Frankie has been drinking consistently ever since we've been married," she stated at the time. "I knew he drank before, but you know, you think things will change." She also claimed that Frankie had struck her when he had been drinking but admitted his blows didn't hurt much. She also claimed Frankie had purchased items such as a washing machine, toaster and jewelry, only to have the items repossessed due to non payment. Betty stated to the press, "The things were all taken back in less than six months." She also mentioned that "he doesn't know how to handle money when he gets it."

Superior Court Judge Arthur Crum granted the divorce. Betty was given custody of their daughter who was six years old at the time. Frankie was ordered to pay $75 a month for Darlene's care. Betty was granted a token $1.00 a month in alimony. The divorce embittered Betty. She had stuck with the marriage for eight years, but Frankie's drinking and money problems finally took their toll. She had also caught Frankie in bed with other women, and more than once, the fact that he brought them into their own apartment infuriated her even more. She would spend the rest of her life regretting their marriage.

With Frankie's film career limited to mostly one day parts at MGM, the $75 a month child support payments would be difficult for him to make. He would attempt to make a few payments, but the little money he did have went to rent, then booze.

Wild Bill hired Frankie for his next film, also released in 1951, entitled *Westward the Women*. The original story was by Frank Capra, who had wanted to direct the film himself, but eventually he sold the property to MGM. The film stars Robert Taylor who has the job of taking a group of mail order brides across country to marry a bunch of cowboys. Frankie has the role of a cowboy who has ordered a bride. At the conclusion, when the woman who is to be Frankie's bride first lays eyes on him she exclaims, "Your picture makes you look taller," Frankie answers, "I'm tall enough!" It's not a big role but with a few days' growth of beard he certainly looks the part and plays it effectively.

With his roles in films becoming less and less important and his salary becoming smaller with each film role, Frankie decided to take another try at a business outside of show business. With his daily drinking to excess it perhaps wasn't a good move to open up a bar, but that's just what he and his friend, ex-agent Lee Carroll, did. The bar was located at 8279 Santa Monica Boulevard in West Hollywood. They named the bar Try Later. On August 16, Frankie announced to the press, "You know when you call Central Casting they tell you only two things on the phone: 'No work' or 'Try Later,'" thus the name of the bar. Frankie also stated at the time, "This is my first venture into this business. I've always wanted to have a bar. I've spent so much money on the other side of bars that I thought I'd get behind one and get even," The Try Later featured a Sunday Morning Club where hungry actors could get a breakfast consisting of ham, eggs, potatoes, toast, coffee and a drink, and all for one dollar. You had to belong to the club however. Frankie stated, "To be a member you've got to have a card and pay a dime. That's to keep out the riffraff." Frankie was no businessman, and the Try Later did not last long. After Frankie and Lee Carroll ended their business arraignment, the bar made headlines in March 1953 when Dorothy Comingore, costar of *Citizen Kane*, was arrested on prostitution charges there. The charges were later dropped when she agreed to enter a clinic for treatment to alcoholism. The bar was apparently one of Veronica Lake's favorite hangouts also.

Frankie's daughter Darlene with his father Frank Darro, Sr.

Frankie lost the bar, but gained a life long companion. With the closing of the Try Later, Frankie began dating Lee Carroll's ex-wife

Dorothy. Frankie would soon begin to introduce Dorothy as his wife, but it's open for speculation if they in fact were ever married. Frankie's daughter Darlene would do research on the matter after her father's death, but could not find any documents to prove a marriage was performed.

Dorothy was a woman of small stature but had a brazen and feisty personality. Although she seemed convinced that before long the studios would call and Frankie would be on top of the game again, Frankie had no such illusions. He knew how the film industry worked all too well, and since the work was getting harder and harder to come by, it was easier just to stay drunk and not have to worry about the next job.

Frankie's next job didn't arrive until the following year, 1952. He would appear in a total of two films, quite a comedown from the years when eight or nine films would be his norm, and with starring or good supporting roles in all of them.

Due to Wellman's influence MGM hired Frankie for these two additional films. First was *The Sellout*, in which he played a character named Little Jake. He's the leader of a jailhouse kangaroo court that fines the film's star (Walter Pigeon) and Whit Bissell for having the audacity to enter their jail. It's a good scene, and Frankie plays it with menacing authority. It's regrettable that it is such a small role. It's also the only film noir in which Frankie ever appeared, and as such it's unfortunate that he couldn't have been cast in similar roles in such films since he could really be menacing when given a chance.

The next film was *Pat and Mike*, starring Spencer Tracy and Katherine Hepburn. Frankie's second assignment with director George Cukor. Frankie plays a caddie in the film that revolves around the world of sports. He has a quick line of dialogue with star Hepburn and he is seen occasionally on the green performing his caddie duties. It became a classic film, but basically it was a nothing role for Frankie, that anyone could have played. For Frankie it simply gave him another hard to come by paycheck.

William Wellman would leave MGM shortly to start work with John Wayne's Batjaq Productions, where he would direct such classics as *The High and the Mighty* and *Island in the Sky*. In the following year, 1953, Frankie would work only one day. The film was the highly forgettable *Siren of Bagdad* that was produced by his former boss Sam Katzman. Frankie is seen as part of an acrobatic team performing for a desert sheik. He does a forward flip, proving that he is as agile as ever. After a raid on the encampment Frankie has one line of dialogue with the star of the movie Paul Henried.

CHAPTER 13
YOU'RE OUT OF LUCK

Frankie had not had a substantial part in a feature in over three years when he joined the cast of *Racing Blood*. This would be the second time that Frankie had appeared in a film with this title, the first being one for Conn back in 1938. The earlier film has no relation to this one, and there was quite a major difference. In the first film, Frankie had top billing; in this film he received tenth billing. This film was produced by the independent company Gateway Pictures and was picked up for release by 20th Century Fox.

The film stars B-movie stalwart Bill Williams, along with Jean Porter and Jimmy Boyd. Frankie plays Ben, a jockey. The story concerns twin colts, one healthy and the other born with a split hoof. The lame colt is ordered destroyed but is saved by the pleadings of a young boy, played by Boyd. The boy nurses the horse until cured, and it winds up winning the big race over its heavily favored twin. Running a scant seventy-five minutes, reviews at the time complained about the film being too long!

Released on May 12, 1954 as a second feature, the movie was quickly forgotten. If it has any distinction today, it's due to the film being released in Cine-color, a cheap color process where the black and white print is actually dipped in color dye to give the film some resemblance of color. Needless to say, this didn't work very well because after a few showings the color dye would start to crack and fall off the print!

Frankie's next job was another independent production, this time with western movie star wannabe Johnny Carpenter. Carpenter was a one man B-western movie factory. He would produce his films, star in them, work on the scripts and then film them in their entirety on his ranch in Sylmar, at the north end of the San Fernando Valley. The ranch was even equipped with its own western town set. Unfortunately for Carpenter, B-westerns had all but dried up by the time he had gotten into the business, but this did not stop the entrepreneur from producing some ultra cheap movies in the genre he loved.

For this production of *The Lawless Rider*, he teamed up with Alex Gordon and the now famous cult movie figure, Edward D. Wood, Jr. who wrote the script and was given associate producer credit. The film was directed by ace stuntman and second unit director, Yakima Canutt, it would be his final credit as a director, since he would spend the rest of his career directing action for big budget films and at the same time becoming a legend in the stunt business.

The story concerns a gang of cattle thieves led by Wood regular, Kenne Duncan. Duncan promises ranch owner Jim Bascom (played by Frankie) untold wealth and power in exchange for half interest in his cattle ranch, which is co-owned by Bascom's sister. Frankie agrees to the bargain and eventually becomes head of Duncan's gang. Johnny Carpenter (playing the good-guy deputy) infiltrates the gang by passing himself off as a famous outlaw. In the final shoot-out Frankie is killed, leaving viewers with the moral lesson that he should have stayed down on the ranch. The film was barely released, but it did afford Frankie with his last substantial costarring role, even though he was paid a paltry $600 for his effort. Also in the cast was Noel Neill, his "girlfriend" from *The Teen Agers* series. Noel would soon join the cast of the *Superman* television series and enter pop culture history.

The Lawless Rider was shown on TV as late as March 1973 by a local Los Angeles station, but it has not been revived like so many of the other Edward D. Wood, Jr. films.

By September 1954, Frankie and Dorothy were living in a small duplex on Dix Street in Hollywood, just blocks from Hollywood Boulevard and off Cahuenga Boulevard, a main artery into downtown Hollywood. The duplex was owned by Dorothy as part of her divorce agreement with her ex-husband. With money problems mounting, Frankie began missing his child support payments. Aware of Frankie's financial condition Betty's current husband offered to fully support Betty and Frankie's daughter Darlene, but Betty went after Frankie anyway. She wanted every last cent owed her. Her animosity toward her ex-husband grew to such an extent that she forbid the use of his name in her house.

Meanwhile, Frankie wrapped up the year with three appearances on the television show *Public Defender*, produced by Hal Roach, Jr. and starring Reed Hadley as the little seen public defender. One episode, entitled *They Never Came Back*, had a few parallels to some of Frankie's current problems. Frankie plays a jockey who is finding it difficult to find employment. He has sunk his nest egg into a restaurant only to see it fail, and he winds up deep in debt. A drawer in his small apartment is filled with pawn tickets. His rival in the episode is none other than Stanley Clements, his costar from *Pride of the Maryland*. Frankie looks a little haggard in the show but still shows the ability to carry off the episode that is built around his character. Unlike real life, however, he is back on top by the end of the episode.

In 1955 Frankie couldn't find any work in film or television. He did find a job as a part time bartender, but he admitted it was a lot more fun on the other side of the bar. On more than one occasion while tending the bar, one of his old movies would pop up on the TV. Then he would have to field questions on why he wasn't working. Frankie was always good natured about it, but one would think it had to bother him.

On August 31, 1955 Frankie was co-guest of honor at a carnival hosted by the Long Beach Sertoma Club, a club that helps deaf children throughout the country. The other honoree was ex-Dead End Kid Bobby Jordan. Jordan had co-starred with Frankie in the Columbia film *Reformatory* back in 1938 and was now having career problems all his own. Jordan's career never did recover after he left the Bowery Boys series in 1947, and he wound up as a door-to-door, kid-on-a-pony photographer before dying of cirrhosis of the liver in 1965 at the age of 43. But at least for one night both actors could forget their career woes and raise some money for a good cause.

CHAPTER 14
FORBIDDEN PLANET

With the market for B movies-as well as many A movies-rapidly evaporating, studios and movie theater owners were in a panic over trying to get audiences to leave their television sets and attend movies once again. Cinemascope, 3-D and Stereophonic Sound were just a few of the methods used to try to lure patrons back. There was also a little used genre that was proving popular with low budget producers-science fiction.

Science fiction films were all the rage during the 1950's. Released in 1950, *Destination Moon* opened the floodgates, and soon every major-and mostly minor-studio released a myriad of outer space epics. Metro Goldwyn Mayer was late in joining the race, but as with most of its films, it did it in a big way!

With a budget of one million dollars, *Forbidden Planet* is a very impressive film. If not the greatest sci-fi epic of the 50's MGM certainly produced, the best looking one. Beautiful Eastman Color and the use of Cinemascope add immeasurably to its over all appeal. The film actually should be seen on the big screen to truly appreciate the fantastic production design, but even on a small television set, the artistry is impressive. With the exception of Anne Francis, who introduced generations of young male sci-fi fans to sexual fantasies, the highlight of the film is Robbie the Robot. Sure, robots had been in films for years, but mostly in serials like the ludicrous robot in *The Phantom Creeps*, or the equally ludicrous one used in *The Monster and the Ape*. Frankie, had his own encounter with robots in *The Phantom Empire* twenty-four years earlier, but for the most part movie robots were phony and cardboard looking in design. For Robbie, MGM hired Bob Kinoshita to design it from rough sketches given him by Disney animator Arnold Gillespie. The finished product was light years ahead of any other cinematic robot. MGM released statements at the time that the robot was filled with wires and was actually operational. In truth, it needed some human help. The interior cavity was just big enough for a small person to fit inside and operate the arms and waist. With size in mind, Frankie fit the bill perfectly.

He stated at the time that he was happy to get the assignment. With the release to television of his old Monogram films, he was quickly becoming something of a TV star. "People started to remember my name," he quipped. As for not actually being seen in the film, he said, "But, I don't mind." "This is a lot of fun," Frankie continued "Besides, I've seen a million people I used to know on the MGM lot. It might lead to regular acting jobs."

Frankie's participation in *Forbidden Planet* has become something of a Hollywood legend but not in a good way, unfortunately. By the time production began in the fall of 1955, Frankie's drinking had also become something of a legend. It was daily, and not just a beer or two. With little work to occupy his time he would drink daily, just to get drunk, plain and simple.

The first day of shooting went fine; however on the second day the problem occurred. After lunch, Frankie was hoisted into Robbie, and was positioned on the transport cart that Robbie uses to ride around in. The scene called for Robbie to exit the cart. When the shot was lined up, the director Fred McLeod called action and Frankie attempted to move Robbie off the cart. Instead of a smooth exit, Frankie stumbled and almost crashed the prized robot to the sound stage floor. Some quick acting stage hands caught Robbie before disaster occurred. Frankie was extracted from Robbie's innards, and it was determined he was drunk. He was promptly fired and was replaced by Frank Carpenter, who finished the film as Robbie.

There are at least two publicity shots showing Frankie, waist high in the Robbie body. In both shots his eyes are covered with a Lone Ranger type mask, but to anyone familiar with Frankie, he would be easily recognizable.

Years later costar Anne Francis stated that at the time she had just assumed Frankie had one too many martinis at lunch. She had no idea that Frankie was at this time in the depths of alcoholism.

In Frankie's defense, the interior of Robbie was not a prime working environment. The suit weighted eighty-four pounds and stood 6'4" tall. With its poor ventilation and close quarters it's been stated that Carpenter would also suffer fainting spells. *Forbidden Planet* costar Richard Anderson stated that "No one should have been inside the robot." He went on to say it simply was not a good working environment inside. Anderson had worked with Frankie on *Across the Wide Missouri* and enjoyed the experience, "Frankie was so much fun, always in a good mood." When Frankie was replaced on *Forbidden Planet* it was a case of he was there and then he was replaced, no explanation was given to the rest of the cast. In any case, MGM did not seem to harbor any grudges. Frankie was back working for them a few months later. Surprisingly, when *Forbidden Planet* was released on March 15, 1956, it did not do well at the box office. It would take years for it to build the following it has today.

Robbie the Robot would also continue to work, without Frankie's participation. In 1957 he would star in the film *Invisible Boy*, and throughout the years pop up on TV shows such as *The Twilight Zone* and *Lost in Space*. As late as 2003, Robbie was seen in a cameo in the Warner Bros. feature *Looney Tunes Back in Action*.

As fate would have it, the scene that Frankie screwed up was never re-shot and does not appear in the finished film.

As mentioned earlier, MGM apparently held no grudges, but the incident could not have done Frankie's career much good. A major star can get away with unacceptable behavior, as long as their films remain popular, but Frankie had little or no clout at this point in his career. When the word gets around that an actor is unreliable, especially due to drinking, producers will look elsewhere when casting for a film or TV show.

Frankie was able to secure a small role in the Cecil B. DeMille extravaganza *The Ten Commandments*, a color Vista Vision remake of his silent screen hit. It was a quick payday for Frankie and nothing more. The opulent looking but hollow spectacle featured hundreds of well known players, some with careers on their way up and others like Frankie, on their way down. It's almost impossible to pick him out in the film. When reminiscing about his participation in the film years later, he would simply tell you, "Yeah, I was in the movie, I played a guard in the palace." Good luck in finding him in the film!

When the film was released by Paramount on October 5, 1956, it became a huge, popular if not critical success, although it would do nothing for Frankie's rapidly fading film career. Most if his fans never knew he was in the film, even if they saw it!

Also in 1956, Frankie showed up on the western TV series *Judge Roy Bean*. The two episodes he appeared in were entitled, *The Cross Draw Kid* and *The Refugee*. It was common practice at the time to use the same cast for two separate episodes, filming them back to back to save money. They would not be broadcast back to back however.

If Frankie was now almost forgotten by the studios, he was still well remembered by some of his fans. In May 1957, entertainment writer Ted Hilgenstuhler and his friend, actor Donn Reed, ran into Frankie at the Hollywood YMCA. Frankie was playing handball, and the two friends chatted with Frankie about his career. When the question came up about what he was currently up to and what had happened to all his money, Frankie answered good naturedly, "I'm doing some TV shows and a few movies...but I'd really like to get into production, as a legman...anything to get started. I'm no different than a lot of old-time actors. Certainly I'm disappointed that I'm not getting any kind of residual payment. But what can I do about it? No, I don't have any money. The courts took it all."

The duo had an idea. Local Los Angeles TV station KTTV had recently started a program entitled *Wallace Berry Theater*. They proposed *The Frankie Darro Theater*, a show aimed at kids and featuring Frankie hosting his own movies, among others. He could also interview actors with whom he had worked through the years. They published their idea in a local TV magazine, even listing Frankie's agent George Ingersol and his phone number in case anyone from a studio would like to pick up on the idea. Sadly nothing came of the idea, but it did have merit.

As mentioned earlier, Frankie would return to MGM in 1957 to film a bit part in its production of *A Tip on a Dead Jockey* starring Dorothy Malone and Robert Taylor. The title is much better than the finished film. The story concerns Taylor getting mixed up with drug smugglers and only turns interesting during the last third of the film, when pilot Taylor is trying to escape capture in his airplane. As

Frankie's career was sinking into oblivion, it was probably appropriate that Frankie plays the title role of the dead jockey and is only seen for about five seconds in the film. He is seen riding a horse against a rear projection screen and then, in a long shot filmed on an actual racetrack, the horse stumbles and Frankie is killed. It's impossible to say if Frankie did the actual stunt himself, but since there is a publicity shot showing him at the track, maybe he earned a couple of extra bucks doing a stunt. The film has a fine score by the always reliable Miklos Rozsa but little else to recommend it.

Frankie's rapidly declining career wasn't his only concern in 1957. In September his ex-wife Betty had him arrested for failing to support their now eleven year old daughter. Frankie was released from jail when a friend posted the $500 bail. Frankie said at the time, "She says I owe her $1,570, but I keep telling her she can't get blood out of a rock. My ex-wife told me she was going to put me in jail, and I said go ahead!" She kept her word. Betty claimed that Frankie had not paid any support for over a year. The trial date was set for October 22. During the trial Frankie admitted that film work had been "very spotty." He said he had worked as a stuntman until he injured his shoulder in a fall the previous year. He also stated that during the previous year he had only made $2,228, and out of his earnings he had to pay his agent $250.

With his personal problems now splashed across various newspapers and his excessive drinking already well known around Hollywood, casting directors and producers had even more reason not to consider Frankie for a role in a movie or television show. And if that was not enough problems for Frankie to handle there was one more to consider. The young people that were now making the casting calls had no idea who Frankie was. If they did, he was thought of as the guy who only played jockeys in those old films that were seen on television.

CHAPTER 15
BLAKE EDWARDS-THE LATE 50'S

With the release of *A Tip on a Dead Jockey* Frankie's feature film career was about finished. A small handful of films would follow, but only one was a decent role for him. Since good parts were difficult to come by, Frankie was reduced to taking any part no matter the size or importance just to keep earning enough money for him and Dorothy to live on.

One temporary salvation in this downward spiral came in the form of writer-director Blake Edwards. Edwards's step-grandfather was silent film director J. Gordon Edwards, and his stepfather was production manager, Jack Edwards. Edwards himself started out as an actor before taking his talents behind the camera. Edwards would utilize Frankie in five projects over the next four years.

First was the Tony Curtis and Janet Leigh comedy, *The Perfect Furlough.* Released in 1958, this comedy concerns Curtis, who's part of a group of servicemen sequestered in the Arctic as part of an experiment in isolation. A lottery is held in which one member of the group would be allowed the perfect furlough. Curtis wheels and deals his way into winning the sole lottery ticket. One of his cons is to play the old shell game with Frankie to win his lottery token. Later, we see Frankie in the infirmary, lying in bed in traction, and of course, Curtis bumps into the bed. This sends Frankie up and off the bed in a twisted mess. At the conclusion of the film Curtis returns to the base, but Frankie is nowhere to be seen. These were only a couple of brief scenes for Frankie, but it was a major studio production by an up and coming, talented writer and director.

Besides being a prolific film director, Edwards moved into television production, not something widely done by successful filmmakers of the time. His premiere series was *Peter Gunn* the noir tinged show set to the rhythms of Henry Mancini, which was an instant hit with the public. The star of the series was Craig Stevens, who played the taciturn Gunn, a private dick who hangs out at a jazz club called Mother's. Gunn would solve cases in the unnamed city between visits to the club and romantic interludes with the club's singer, played by sultry Lola Albright.

Frankie had the title role in the thirteenth episode entitled, *The Jockey*. The original story was written by Edwards himself. In the episode Frankie plays a world famous Jockey named Billy Arnett. Arnett's wife has died, and he thinks she was murdered. Arnett hires Gunn to discover the truth. Frankie has two extended scenes in the show, but more importantly, the entire episode revolves around his character. Age and hard living has certainly caught up with Frankie, but his energy level is high, and his raspy voiced delivery is perfect for the part. The episode premiered on December 15, 1958. The episode was included in A&E's DVD release of *Peter Gunn* in 2002. Even though his personal life had disintegrated due to his drinking at the time, the episode proves that Frankie was still capable of a sustained performance of more than just a few seconds of screen time, if he could only find someone willing to take the chance and hire him.

Operation Petticoat-1959.

Blake Edwards' feature follow up to *The Perfect Furlough* was another service comedy entitled *Operation Petticoat*. The film was based on an original story by former Loyola football player Paul King and Joseph Stone, who claimed they based their story on actual incidents during World War II.

Frankie and Tony Curtis on the set of *Operation Petticoat*-1959.

Told in flashback, the film concerns the crew of the submarine USS Sea Tiger and its mission to return a group of stranded nurses safely back to port in the Pacific during World War II. Cary Grant and Tony Curtis are the male leads, with Joan O'Brien and Dina Merrill as the main nurses. The film is full of fine character actors such as, Gene

Evans, Arthur O'Connell and Gavin MacLeod. Frankie is billed sixteenth and plays Dooley, the pharmacist's mate, the same position he held during his own stint in the Navy during World War II. Frankie, looking grizzled, is a joy to watch. He fits the part perfectly and, although visible aged, still exhibits the high energy level of his earlier days. At one point Gene Evans (playing Molumphry) spots the group of beautiful nurses about to board the sub. He turns to Frankie and states, "If anyone asks what you're fighting for, there's your answer." Frankie removes his sailor cap, holds it over his heart and gives a hilarious comic leer.

Frankie pops up throughout the film. At one point he is seen patching up burns on Cary Grant's butt and later is seen relaxing in his bunk until the Captain (played by Grant) enters and yells at him. Then Frankie bolts out of bed and hits his head on the low ceiling above. Still later in the film, the crew is having a luau topside, and Frankie is seen being carried on a pole by two sailors, ala a pig, about to be roasted. The party is broken up by a Japanese air attack.

Filming began in March 1959 and wrapped 28 days later on April 28. Frankie fondly remembered the shoot as one of the most pleasant times of his life. Most of the filming was done in Florida, far away from his problems back in Hollywood, and it was more like a vacation for him. He stayed at The Blue Marlin Hotel in Key West. Since most of his films were shot in the studio, it was a real treat to go away on location. The weather was warm and comfortable, and between breaks in the filming Frankie would amaze the cast and crew by taking comic dives off the bow of the submarine being used for the movie. For the duration of the film he was able to forget about all the problems back in Hollywood.

The film was screened for the press in November and released to the public in Los Angeles on December 25. The Universal release became a huge hit, grossing $6.8 million, putting it behind only *Ben-Hur* and *Psycho* for the highest grossing film of 1960. It was nominated for one Academy Award, for best story and screenplay written directly for the screen but failed to win the coveted award.

As successful as the film was-and it's still fondly remembered today, the part did not lead to any other substantial supporting roles for

Frankie. Frankie's feature film career had just slipped into oblivion. There would be other roles, but nothing on the scale of *Operation Petticoat.*

Later in 1959 Frankie was hired to perform stunts in a film being produced by Walt Disney entitled *Darby O'Gill and the Little People*. The film starred a young Sean Connery and Janet Munro. Frankie was the stunt double for actor Jimmy O'Dea (who portrayed King Brian, the King of the Leprechauns). Early on in the film Frankie gets to perform one of his trademark back flips, and then later in the film he does a long jump, assisted by wires, that has him crashing into a huge prop door. After seeing the rushes of that scene, Disney asked his assistant the name of the actor performing that stunt. "Frankie Darro," he answered. Disney shot back "Is he still with us?" Through the years the film has become a family classic for Disney just as *Pinocchio* had.

With the successful television series *Peter Gunn* still filming, Edwards produced yet another show entitled, *Mr. Lucky*, based on the 1943 Cary Grant film of the same name. The series was built around well known gambler Mr. Lucky, owner of a gaming ship that conveniently stayed beyond the twelve mile limit to avoid problems with the authorities. Mr. Lucky was played by square jawed John Vivyan, and Henry Mancini again supplied the music.

In the episode entitled *The Big Squeeze* Frankie plays the part of The Jockey, supposedly "the best wheel man in the business." The plot has Mr. Lucky being framed for an armored car robbery he didn't commit. Frankie is first glimpsed looking over his shoulder from behind the wheel of a gateway car. Moments after an off screen explosion, he steps on the gas to escape the scene of the crime with his accomplices. When Mr. Lucky finally catches up the Jockey and grabs him by the lapels of his coat he hoists Frankie to his own eye level. Frankie demands to be put down, and when he is he states, "I hate big guys. If there is anything in the world I hate, it's big guys!" Frankie, looking rather haggard, brings an effective mix of toughness and sarcasm to the two minute scene. After watching his performance, it's not difficult to imagine him playing the gunsel in *The Maltese Falcon.*

The episode was produced and directed by cult favorite Jack Arnold and has the same noir look as a *Peter Gunn* episode, probably due to cinematographer Philip Lathrop, who also worked on *Peter Gunn*. However, *Mr. Lucky* was not as successful as *Peter Gunn* and it was canceled after its first season.

Frankie and Blake Edwards would cross paths one final time in late 1961. Edwards and Larry Gelbart wrote the screenplay for the comedy-mystery *The Notorious Landlady* directed by Richard Quine and starring Jack Lemmon, Kim Novak and Fred Astaire. The film was set in England but for the most part was filmed in Southern California. The ending takes place in a beautiful seaside resort for seniors. Lemmon and Novak must locate an old woman (played by veteran Estelle Winwood) before she is killed by a supposed friend. Lemmon spots her just as the wheelchair bound Winwood is about to be shoved off a cliff, high above the ocean. The sequence of Lemmon chasing after the wheelchair goes on for some time. Frankie was hired to be the stunt double for Winwood. As scary as the sequence looks, with shots of the wheelchair zooming down a dirt path on its way to the cliff and eventually the sea below, it was all highly choreographed. The wheelchair was on cables to prevent it from actually running away. The only glimpses of Frankie we see are of his arms and legs flailing away as the wheelchair careens out of control. What was supposed to be a beautiful seaside in England was actually Carmel, California.

With the release of *The Notorious Landlady*, Frankie's association with Blake Edwards came to an end. Edwards career, however, would soar throughout the sixties and beyond with the release of such classics as *Breakfast at Tiffany's* and *The Pink Panther* series. With less and less work coming his way Frankie could spend even more time in the bars along Hollywood Boulevard.

CHAPTER 16
THE 1960'S

The country and indeed the world were in the mood to party on December 31, 1959. It was time to close out the conservative decade of the 1950's and look forward to the 1960's. Seventy million children, known as Baby Boomers, would soon be teenagers and young adults, changing the face of the nation forever. Frankie was in the mood to celebrate also. He celebrated that New Year's Eve by getting drunk, not a new occurrence by any means, but this time he stripped naked and ran down the streets of Long Beach, California. His impromptu celebration came to an abrupt end with the arrival of the Long Beach Police. He got to sleep off the booze in the city jail.

Something else happened on January 1, 1960 that profoundly affected Frankie, along with every other actor carrying a Screen Actors Guild Card. Since the advent of television, the question of residuals had raised its ugly head. The studios were making a fortune showing their old films on television and not paying out a cent in residuals because the talent at the time was paid on a per film or per year contract. Some of the actors sued to keep their films off TV but to little avail. After years of negotiations, the resolution came down to this: the studios could keep all profits from all movies and TV shows produced prior to April 1, 1960, but shows completed after that date would require residual payments of a gradually lessening scale. Actors with careers like Frankie's were basically screwed. With his old films popping up constantly on late night TV, he could only watch and shake his head with disappointment. There would be no check in the mail for him, although it would be a windfall for those actors who could stay active in the business. Unfortunately, Frankie was not among those actors able to stay very active.

With little hope of substantial film work on the horizon, Frankie's wife Dorothy went looking for work. She found a job at Addie's, a popular children's clothing store on Hollywood Boulevard within walking distance of the hotel room they now shared. She would stay employed there for the next twenty-five years. Once in a while the phone would ring for Frankie, and he would sober up and go back to work. On February 25, 1960 he appeared on the popular ABC television show *The Untouchables*. It was only one day's worth of work, but Frankie still had it in him to turn in a good performance. Graying and weathered as a newspaper vendor during the opening minutes of the show, he looks older than his forty-two years but certainly fits the part. Perhaps the most amazing aspect of his appearance is his stature. During the episode Frankie is standing on an off-camera platform of some kind, which makes him look about five inches taller. The episode entitled *The Unhired Assassin* was initially shown in two parts and eventually reedited and released to theaters as *The Guns of Zangora*. It's unfortunate that it was a one time performance since it's the kind of role that could have lent itself to becoming a running part.

Later that same year a tribute to sorts was paid to Frankie by, of all people, Lenny Bruce, popular and controversial comedian who released a record of a live concert. The performance featuring a takeoff on Warner Bros. gangster films. At one point in the album, he rattles off names of a make believe film, mentioning such Warner Bros. stalwarts as "Charles Bickford, Barton MacLane, George E. Stone and Frankie Darro." Frankie was unaware of this mention until twelve years later. When told about it, he smiled and seemed truly touched by the small tribute.

On May 15, 1960 Frankie showed up on an episode of the television show *Alfred Hitchcock Presents*. The episode, entitled *I Can Take Care of Myself*, concerns a two bit gangster by the name of Little Dandy (played by Frankie) who has desires on a thrush at a local nightclub. The singer, named Georgia, is played by Linda Lawson. Little Dandy's advances are rebuffed by her piano player, Bert Haber (played by Myron McCormick). Since Little Dandy doesn't take rebuffs kindly, he sets a trap to capture the piano player. Frankie, spiffily dressed in a dark suit and wearing a white carnation, plays a wonderfully ruthless gangster. His voice is raspier than usual, most probably due to his heavy drinking and smoking. At one point in the show Georgia dumps a drink on his head, and Little Dandy takes a fall over a table. Frankie also did the stunt, making it as realistic as possible. Unfortunately, Frankie's heavy consumption of alcohol was not just taking its toll on his looks and voice. Early in the show after Georgia finishes a song, Frankie raises his cocktail glass to toast her performance. His hand is visibly shaking. Unfortunately the show isn't very effective. The plot twist at the end is pretty much of a letdown and it didn't have on O'Henry type of ending the show was known for. When the piano player enters what he believes is a detective's car, the man in the back seat, hidden behind a newspaper, is one of Little Dandy's henchmen. For whatever reason, they didn't use Frankie, it would have been much more effective to have Frankie himself sitting there.

Frankie and Linda Lawson from an episode of *Alfred Hitchcock Presents*-1960.

After substantial parts in the *Mr. Lucky* episode, as discussed earlier, and *Alfred Hitchcock Presents*, Frankie found it even more difficult to find work and he didn't work at all in 1961. He and Dorothy continued to live in a small hotel room in Hollywood, with Dorothy bringing in enough money for a little food and lots of alcohol for both of them. An occasional residual check for Frankie's post 1960's performance would provide some additional cash, but there was no telling when one would arrive and for what amount. On rare occasions Frankie's daughter Darlene would make the trip up from Long Beach with friends from her high school to visit her once famous father. Since Frankie's alcohol intake had long diminished his abilities to be a concerned or involved father, the visits were infrequent. Frankie's wife Dorothy was also a problem. She wanted Frankie all for herself and didn't appreciate visits from other women, even if the other women were his only daughter.

Early in 1962 the phone rang once again. Frankie was wanted for another episode of *Alfred Hitchcock Presents*. The episode was entitled, *Ten O'Clock Tiger*. The show was simply plotted but effective. "Doc" Murphy (played by Frankie) has acquired a serum that revitalizes a worn out race horse into winning a race. Doc convinces a boxing trainer (played by Robert Keith) to use it on Soldier Fresno, a washed up boxer he's been fronting. The serum works, turning the has been into a contender. Before the big title fight Keith gives the pugilist a bigger dose than normal to insure a win. But, Soldier Fresno goes wild and beats Keith to death in the dressing room. The show proves that as late as 1962 Frankie still can turn in a fully realized performance. With his overly raspy voice and constant puffing on cigarettes there is a real sense of dread in his performance. Sure, Frankie looks worn, to the point of worn out actually and at least a decade older than his forty-four years, but this does help his characterization. Frankie delivers the rapid fire dialogue without missing a beat, in the same punchy style that he did for Monogram, and his worn appearance actually improves in the second half of the episode. Unfortunately, the show would mark the final appearance of Frankie in a role of any substance or a role that required anything other than a couple of quick lines. For all intensive purposes, his days as a working actor would be over, now leaving even more time to hit the bottle.

Frankie on The Red Skelton Show. This photo was one of Frankie's favorites. It hung on his wall for years.

As often happens with actors, a job came to Frankie out of the blue. Comedian Red Skelton had a long running and inexplicably popular television variety show. It basically appealed to rural audiences, but the show stayed in the top ten for most of its twenty year run. Skelton had publicly admitted that he was an alcoholic who had now given up drinking. He hired Frankie for the show on one condition. Frankie would stay on the show as long as he didn't show up drunk. In one show in October 1962 Frankie worked with Jackie Coogan. When Coogan commented to a reporter that Frankie had played loads of crooked jockey roles, Frankie retorted, "I played so many crooked jockeys that they paid me by the furlong!"

For Skelton Frankie would appear in various sketches, most notably, dressed as an old woman, doing his trademark back flips and prat falls. Frankie brought his young daughter to the taping of one of the shows and on this particular show with Frankie was Lassie. His owner, Rudd Weatherwax, gave Darlene a puppy as a gift. On an episode broadcast in April 1963, Frankie plays a dental patient to Skelton's dentist. Skelton tries to remove Frankie's stubborn tooth in the pantomime sketch.

As records are sketchy, it's impossible to say exactly how many shows he actually appeared in, but his final regular appearance was recorded as March 16, 1965. Apparently, Frankie had shown up for work drunk, and true to his word, Skelton had fired him. Ace Republic stuntman David Sharpe replaced Frankie. Skelton must have had a change of heart a few years later, because he hired Frankie again on a one time basis in 1968.

During the mid 1960's a popular carnival occupied the corner of Pico Boulevard and La Cienega. The carnival featured rides and a petting zoo stocked with goats, pigs and even a monkey. To earn some much needed cash for Dorothy and him, Frankie got a job there. Perhaps to disguise himself from the few who would recognize him, he grew a beard. Working at the carnival no doubt brought back happy memories of his days in the circus. The job didn't last long, most likely due to Frankie's drinking, but it did pay a few bills while it lasted.

As the lean years rolled on, Frankie would continue to spring for the $15 needed every year to keep his picture and phone number in The Academy Players Directory. The large soft bound book includes contact information on hundreds of actors, and is issued three times a year to casting directors, among others, by The Academy of Motion

Pictures Art and Sciences. It did little good for Frankie. He would also keep his name and phone number in the Hollywood phone book. If you needed Frankie, he was always easy to contact. Unfortunately, no one seemed to need him.

Late in 1962 he picked up one day's work as a delivery man on an episode of the talking horse sit-com *Mr. Ed* and then another day's work as an elevator operator on the television version of *Going My Way*, based on the popular RKO movie from 1944. It would be another two years before Frankie was able to find even a day's worth of work in front of the cameras.

Frankie's name made it to the local gossip column in June 1963 when a friend spotted Frankie standing in line at the unemployment office. The friend asked Frankie, "How come your agent doesn't keep you working?" Frankie replied, "Don't ask me, ask my agent. He's standing in line directly behind me. He's collecting too!"

In 1964 Frankie worked for one day in the Paramount feature *The Carpetbaggers*, a sprawling soap opera about a Howard Hughes-type tycoon, who winds up owning a movie studio. The film's chief assets are Elmer Bernstein's powerful score and Carroll Baker, especially when she's dressed in revealing lingerie. The film was quite controversial when initially released due in large part to its casual sexual morals. Frankie (playing a bellboy) shows up after eighty-six minutes of the one hundred and fifty minute film. He is seen hauling a rack of fur coats in George Peppard's hotel suite where he has two lines, one upon entering the suite, "Yes, Mr. McCord" and one upon leaving, "Thank you, Mr. McCord." These would be Frankie's final lines of dialogue in a major motion picture. His scene lasts for just under one minute.

Popular comedian Jerry Lewis was in production with his film *Disorderly Orderly* when *The Carpetbaggers* was released. After a day of filming Lewis invited some of the cast and crew over to his home for a screening of the film. By the way, the cast included, the son and daughter of his favorite director William Wellman, William Wellman, Jr. and Cissy Wellman. As the screening progressed, Frankie's scene came on and Jerry Lewis jumped to his feet and yelled, "Is that Frankie Darro?" Someone yelled out in the affirmative. "Stop the projector!" Lewis yelled. "I want Frankie Darro in our film." One of the executives reminded Lewis that the film had already been cast. "I don't care," Lewis commanded. "I want him in the film." Jerry got his way and a place was found for Frankie in the film. Say what you want about his ability as a comedian, but Jerry did remember the character actors and stars of yesterday.

In the movie, Frankie is seen sitting at a meeting of hospital administrators, pounding his knuckles into the table in agreement with what is being spoken, in unison with the others at the table. It's a silent bit, but Frankie looks tan and healthy and sharp, dressed in a suit and a tie. Jerry Lewis became one of Frankie's favorite film makers.

Also in 1964 another tribute of sorts was paid to Frankie, one that he was never aware of. Hanna-Barbera Studios, producers of animated TV shows such as *The Flintstones* and *Top Cat*, hired animator Doug Wildey to devise a television first, a prime time animated adventure show inspired by the Tom Swift novels and the comic strip "Terry and the Pirates", among others. The show featured a young boy named Jonny Quest, an adventurous lad who was in and out of trouble on a regular basis. Jonny fought mummies, space invaders, and you name it. Wildey based the character Jonny on Frankie and to a lesser extent, Jackie Coogan. Viewing the show, entitled *Jonny Quest*, you can see the influence Frankie's screen persona had, if only in the way Jonny is quick to act, then once in a predicament, must quickly act again to extricate himself from some dire situation, most often with the help of an adult.

In the winter of 1964 Frankie was hired to play a role as an elevator operator on TV's *Perry Mason*. The following year he was seen briefly as a delivery man on *The Addams Family,* which gave Frankie the opportunity to work again with Jackie Coogan the once popular child star. Coogan's career had hit the skids years earlier, but his career was resurrected thanks to the hit show. In 1966 Frankie worked one day in the role of a newspaper vendor on the popular television show *Batman*. In 1967 he had another one day job on the western television series *The Guns of Will Sonnett*, where he played a bartender. The following year, Jerry Lewis called again. He had a one day silent bit for Frankie, as a deliveryman in his film *Hook Line and Sinker*. The film would mark a further decline in Lewis's own work.

To pass the time Frankie enjoyed staying up late and watching television. He would never attend the movies. He just didn't care for the direction current cinema was taking, but watching an old film or a current TV show was entertainment enough for him. He especially liked *The Tonight Show*, starring Johnny Carson. On occasion Carson would mention Frankie's name in his skit Tea Time Movies. Frankie had never met Carson, but he did appreciate the mention. He would stay up watching the tube until the booze took its desired effect and sent him off to sleep. Occasionally, when someone would recognize Frankie at a bar or on the street, the same question would inevitably be asked, "Hey Frankie, why don't we see you on the screen anymore?" "I got no answer for that," he said at the time.

In April 1969 a magazine was published entitled "Good Old Days-The Magazine of Happy Memories". By 1969 the Vietnam War had escalated and protests were in the media along with depressing news of the war as casualties were high. Looking back at happy memories brought readers a needed break. A feature of the magazine was "Remember Those Movie Kids" by Harry Wilkinson. It featured a portrait of young Frankie, along with a short biography. Frankie was now relegated to being a product of the good old days, an answer to a nostalgia question. As the decade came to a close, he celebrated another birthday. He was fifty-two years old, broke, unemployed and fighting the effects of hangovers on an almost daily basis.

CHAPTER 17
THE 1970'S

The Hollywood that Frankie knew in his days of stardom of the 1930's and '40's has ceased to exist long ago. Hollywood had been going through massive changes, not just the studios, but the town itself. The days of seeing glamorous movie stars shopping in exclusive shops along Hollywood Blvd., had been replaced by sights of hookers and drug dealers blatantly plying their trade in the open for all to see. The photochemical smog that had choked Los Angeles for decades would reach its zenith in the 70's. Smog alerts were an almost daily occurrence during the hot summer months. The thick eye-reddening smog would blanket the famous boulevard, making it difficult to see across the street, but if you consider the street life, it was not necessarily a bad thing.

The studios were in financial ruin. Twentieth Century Fox, still reeling from the beating it took on *Cleopatra*, along with other bad investments sold off its back lot to avoid certain bankruptcy. Fox took what money it made and invested in other mega budget flops like *Hello Dolly*, and *Darling Lili*. MGM held an auction to sell off its old props, and then promptly also sold off its back lot for more cash.

Movie attendance was at an all time low. In 1970 only 17.5 million people attended movie theaters weekly, down from 44 million only five years earlier. Theater owners were closing shop, selling off their beloved movie palaces, which in turn were torn down and replaced by new businesses or parking lots. The theater owners who stayed with the business were fighting the unknown entity called Pay TV, something they were certain would surely seal their collective doom. Studios with names such as FBO, Sono Art-World Wide, Mascot and Monogram were just dusty memories for the few who could remember their output. Their once famous stars were equally forgotten.

The ancillary markets for older films, such as video tapes, discs and cable TV, just didn't exit yet. Cable stations like TCM or AMC, which would turn film libraries into gold mines, were still in the future.   Paramount Studios, so certain of the low value of its pre-1950 film library, had sold it to Universal.   Except for movies with the cult stars of the time like Bogart or W.C. Fields, the films of the golden age of Hollywood were considered dead-weight.

As the 1970's began, Frankie and Dorothy were living at the St. Francis Hotel at 5533 Hollywood Blvd.   Like the rest of the boulevard, the once elegant building, had become a seedy looking dump, populated by transients and drunks, a place where only the down and out would bother to enter and even they would proceed with caution. Across the street sat a long closed building that had once housed the famed Lawlor Professional School that Frankie had attended in his better days.   Legend has it that during the golden age in Hollywood, the St. Francis was connected by an underground tunnel to production offices across the street so executives could meet their mistresses for a quick tryst.   If the tunnel did in fact exist, no longer was it in use. More importantly now for Frankie, the St. Francis Hotel was around the corner from Holly-West Liquor on Western Ave., easy walking distance when he had only a few bucks to spend on a bottle of booze.

Prospects for work had looked dim for years now for Frankie. However a couple of job possibilities appeared on the horizon, both of which came about thanks to his old buddy Mantan Moreland.   Mantan had suffered a serious stroke in New York back in 1958, and sadly, when he was able to work again, his persona was out of favor.   His type of comedy was lumped in with the likes of Stepin' Fetchit and Sleep 'N Eat. No one was bothering to take a closer look at how brilliant the man could be.   However, by the late 1960's and early 70's he was finally being recognized for the comic genius he was.   He began appearing on shows like *Julia* and *The Bill Crosby Show*. Illness had taken its toll, but Mantan had gathered his strength and taken a new partner, Roosevelt Myles, who used the last name Livingood, while performing.   They were appearing at night clubs and on TV shows such as *The Merv Griffin Show*.

Mantan was also hired to star in a pilot for a proposed TV show entitled *Time for Mantan*.   If the program was picked up, Mantan had a running part for Frankie.   He stated at the time how important Frankie had been in getting his contract at Monogram.   Mantan's hiring had broken the color barrier at Monogram. "He's a wonderful man. He really fought for me," he said, talking of his old friend. Sadly, the show was not picked up. Even if it had been, it's very doubtful that Frankie would have been able to sustain the grind of a weekly show. Since his life now was all wrapped around the bottle.

Mantan was able to secure employment for Frankie from a most unusual source, the USO. Mantan and his comedy partner Roosevelt Livingood had been booking themselves with the USO for some time. They had even booked a tour to Vietnam in early 1970. A tour of war torn Vietnam might seem like a dicey proposition for the frail sixty-eight year old comic, but he was willing to take the chance. Unfortunately, just before the trip, his health took a turn for the worse, and he was forced to back out. Not wanting to spoil the gig for his partner, he suggested Frankie as a replacement. Frankie had apparently been a supporter of the divisive war and gladly stepped in to replace his friend. So he and Livingood flew off to Vietnam.

Frankie in Vietnam. His partner Roosevelt Livingood is on his left.

They entertained troops at bases as diverse as the 5th Special Forces Camp at Pleiku (located far inland, just a few hundred miles from Cambodia), Buon Me Thuot (located south of Pleiku) and also Tuy Hoa and Nha Trang (located on the coast of the South China Sea). The lodgings were sparse for the duo. During their stay at the King Duy Hotel in early April, they shared a room for $3.00 a night.

One of Frankie's final head shots.

The photos that survive of this tour show Frankie and Livingood surrounded by young soldiers, all smiling and enjoying each other's company. With the exception of one photo, which has Frankie looking hung over and sporting a sore or bruise on his lower lip, Frankie always appears smiling, hale, and clear eyed, albeit with his ever present cigarette in hand.

The soldiers for the most part would have been too young to remember Frankie in his heyday, but the looks of enjoyment on their faces show that Frankie and Livingood made an impact with their show. Both deserve credit for their willingness to tour Vietnam. The war was in full force during their visit, and at home the tide was turning away from supporting the war. Just as few months before the duo left for their tour, 250,000 people protested the war in Washington, DC, and upon his return Frankie had his own change of heart in his support of the controversial war. He promptly removed the pro-Vietnam posters that had lined the walls of his hotel room. He stated at the time, "I learned a lot I didn't know about what we've done over there. It's a dirty, filthy war and I want no more part of it!" Frankie's short employment with the USO ended with his trip to Vietnam.

Dorothy continued to work at the clothing store not far from the hotel where they lived, but work for Frankie at this time was non existent. Nothing makes an actor more worried than absolutely no hint of work on the horizon, especially an actor with almost fifty years in the business. Frankie's way of dealing with the situation was to go out and hit the local bars again. By early afternoon nearly every day and depending on how much cash or credit was available to him, Frankie would make his way out of the hotel to walk around the streets of East Hollywood, checking out various dives in search of a drink. Occasionally someone would recognize him and offer to buy him a drink in his honor. That was a good day.

CHAPTER 18
THE WORST OF HOLLYWOOD

In June of 1972, I drove down to Hollywood from my home in the San Francisco Bay Area. Along for the ride was my friend from high school Steve Monzo. We both lived and breathed films, especially classic films from the 1930's. Laurel and Hardy, Cagney, the Universal monster movies-we watched and loved them all. I had just graduated from high school and was working part time at a local movie theater, and my boss, another avid film buff, had given us addresses of various celebrities to look up once we arrived in L.A. Our intention was to look up as many of these celebrities as possible. Frankie Darro's address was included on our list. My boss said to be sure and look him up because he was always happy to sign autographs. We were well armed with stills, for them to sign.

Frankie and the author, John Gloske-June 1972.

As this was long before celebrity stalkers, this idea was not as far fetched as it might sound today. We had the home addresses of stars such as Raymond Massey, James Stewart, Groucho Marx, and Randolph Scott, along with directors Fritz Lang and Rouben Mamoulian. In our young minds we thought they would be more than happy to greet out of town fans. And surprisingly, most were. The key was in telling them we had come all the way from the San Francisco Bay Area. Everyone seemed to love San Francisco. The one notable exception to our plan was Raymond Massey, who slammed the door in my face! Since he walked with a cane and was wearing a bathrobe, I figured he was justified.

Sorry, Mr. Massey.

We stayed at Steve's aunt and uncle's house in Redondo Beach, and each day we would make our sojourn into Hollywood, diligently checking the map in our search for each home. Frankie's was the easiest to find. The St. Francis Hotel sat ominously on Hollywood Boulevard, just west of Western Avenue, quite a difference from the homes in Beverly Hills we had just visited. But being young and open for any adventure, we parked the car and made our way into the hotel. When we entered, we were slightly intimidated by the appearance of the place. It looked like the kind of hotel that had seen lots of trouble over the years, but as we were fearless and determined, not much would have stopped us on our quest. Anyway, we walked to the front desk, and the clerk on duty told us to call Frankie on the house phone, located in a nearby closet. It was the oldest phone I had ever seen. Upon emerging from the closet, I announced to Steve that I had indeed spoken with Frankie Darro and he had invited us up to his room. We entered the elevator, not entirely positive it would reach its destination. Happily, it did, and when the door opened Frankie was standing there to greet us wearing only an undershirt and boxer shorts. However, he had a big grin on his face and extended his hand in friendship saying, "Hi, you don't recognize me, but I'm Frankie Darro." He escorted us into his small room and we sat down in the living room while he went into the bedroom to get fully dressed. In these years before home video, I only knew of Frankie's work from the *Bowery Boys* films that

I watched religiously every Saturday afternoon. I had brought some stills from those films for him to autograph. Upon his return we explained to him our mission in Los Angeles, to track down as many celebrities as possible for autographs. He seemed to take delight in what we were doing. When he learned we were from the San Francisco Bay Area, he really seemed to warm up to us. San Francisco turned out to be one of his favorite cities as well. He stated that people were friendlier there. I can't claim it to be true, but for Frankie it was. He also told us that his father lived in a room on the floor just above him. This surprised us. We couldn't conceive that his father was still alive since we had figured that Frankie was much older than he actually was. After the conversation had slowed a bit, Frankie offered to show us some of his personal memorabilia, from deep in the closet he pulled out a cardboard orange crate filled with what I would consider to be Holy Grail for film buffs (well, this film buff anyway). We sat shocked and enthralled as he showed us autographed stills of Boris Karloff, John Barrymore, The Marx Brothers, Bette Davis, and many more of the other stars he had worked with over the years. A still from Madge Evans was signed, "To Frankie, The Mayor of Hell, Good Luck and Best Wishes from Madge Evans." All the pictures were in fact dedicated to Frankie, in warm tribute from the stars of yesterday. Also in the box was a yellowing newspaper that featured the premiere of *Wild Boys of the Road*. The photos showed people lining around the block to enter the theater. He was understandably proud of the film. He told us it was his favorite of all his films, and he really wanted us to see it. We assured him that we would watch for it on TV.

By the looks of the surrounding apartment, one could easily tell that this box was all that Frankie had left of his career and its contents were quite possibly, with the exception of some clothes, the only possessions of any kind he had left in the world.

We spent a couple of hours in rapt attention, listening to him tell stories of his days as a working actor. We would throw out a name, say Jimmy Cagney, and Frankie would tell us what a great guy he was. It seemed to us that Frankie thought everyone he worked with was a nice guy or gal. We begged Frankie to tell us some "dirt," tell us stories of sex and well more sex-tell us the racy stories. He wouldn't do it. I got the impression that Frankie felt he was a member of an exclusive club, and though his membership had long since been canceled, he was not going to bring dishonor to the club. The only time he broke his rule is when the name Mary Beth Hughes came up. "Don't get me started on her!" he shouted. I never did learn what the problem was. They never made a movie together. She spent the majority of her career in B films just like Frankie so their paths could have crossed. She also appeared in a few Red Skelton shows, so perhaps that's where the animosity came from. Eventually, we said our goodbyes with a promise to keep in touch. He told us to visit him any time we were in town. We told him we planned to return later in the summer.

On our way back home a few days later, we talked about how we couldn't believe our luck. We now had a movie star as a friend-okay, a down-on-his-luck, out-of-work movie star, but still we considered him our friend! We also were amazed by his very positive attitude. Here was a man living in a flophouse of a hotel and by the looks of the place he was probably broke. But he was so cheerfully positive. We couldn't wait to tell our friends back home of our good luck.

About three months later, Steve and I decided to take a trek back to Los Angeles. During this visit we met Frankie's wife Dorothy. There has always been a debate whether they were actually married or not, but Frankie always referred to her as his wife. To put it kindly, our visits always went better when Dorothy was not present. She seemed to have some kind of control over Frankie, and she tried to exert that same control over the people around her, namely Steve and I. When she was around, the conversation was about her. She looked on us suspiciously, as if we were after Frankie's money. Of course, he had none. She would drink in front of us, Frankie would disappear into his room for a little while, and then reappear a few minutes later with the smell of alcohol on his breath, but he never drank in front of us. She also liked to argue. Anything would set her off. Frankie would calm her down, but after a few minutes she would star up again. In her mind Frankie was still a big star, and the next starring role was just a phone call away.

As I said, it was just better when she wasn't around. Sometimes when we didn't see her, I got the feeling that there had been a big fight and she had left, but she would be back again the next visit. One night she was thankfully gone. We took Frankie across the street to The Sizzler for dinner. We were delighted to take him out and sensed that he rarely ate at restaurants afterwards, back in his hotel room, we sat by his window and watched while a film crew was staging a car chase. The scene called for a car to flip over, but try as they might, the car just would not flip properly. Frankie said it was no big deal and then went into explaining the fine points of how to properly flip a car over. When I suggested that he go down and tell them how to do it, Frankie looked at me and said, "No, let them do it. I've had my time. Now it's their time and they have to figure it out on their own."

Frankie at The Cinema Shop in San Francisco.

The Cinema Shop in San Francisco was like Mecca for local film buffs. The owner, Dan Faris, sold movie posters, stills and other memorabilia and held court over an ever expanding group of film enthusiasts who would hang around his shop and talk for hours on end about all things pertaining to cinema, new and old, well known and obscure. Dan was always cooking up ideas on how to make a quick buck and finally decided to produce a television show. The show was eventually called *The Worst of Hollywood* and featured public domain B films along with guests. The show was hosted by Dan's friend Bob Daniels. For the first show his guest was none other than John Carradine, but the guests on succeeding shows were a sorry lot. He had guests like Bill Rae, a local San Francisco character who I'm not sure to this day really appeared in any of the films and television shows he claimed to be in. Dan even used me on one show. I was instructed to tell the audience what it was like to have grown up next to Zorro, the son of the canine star Rin Tin Tin. A totally fabricated story, but I did keep a straight face while being interviewed on the subject. It was that kind of show. When the production started to make a little money, Dan started to look around for another guest of Carradine's stature to add a little class to the show. I mentioned to Dan that I could probably get Frankie if he was interested. He liked the idea and ran it past the station manager. The station manager happened to be a fan of Frankie's and loved the idea even more than Dan did.

Dan also had another idea. He hadn't been pleased with Daniels' hosting of the show. So he asked me if I thought Frankie could possibly host it on a weekly basis. He proposed to fly Frankie in once a week to tape the show, and then fly him home the same day. I called Frankie and ran all this by him. His answer was a resounding, "Yes!" Everyone was excited by this prospect. The plan was to have him tape one regular show, hosted by Daniels, and then shoot another show with Frankie as the host. If it worked, Frankie would have a steady job. I was especially excited, since I had put the deal together. If it all worked out, I would reap some financial reward (to be determined at a later date), and better still, Steve and I would have some sort of position on the show.

Steve and I picked Frankie and Dorothy up from Oakland Airport on Friday morning. The show was to be taped on Saturday. Dorothy was a last minute addition. She had not been part of the original deal until a few days before when Frankie stated that she must come along. Steve and I were not happy about this, but that's the way it was to be. Their fifty-five minute flight went fine. We explained to Frankie that we had a nice hotel waiting for them but that first we wanted to take him by the set and show him what Dan had created. He was all for it, but since Dorothy wanted to rest at the hotel, we dropped her off before proceeding to the television studio. Dan had created an impressive looking set decorated with movie posters from his collection, many featuring Frankie. Frankie was eager for the opportunity to appear on the show, and we were all looking forward to the taping scheduled for early the following morning. Dan suggested that we all meet at The Cinema Shop to show Frankie around so he could meet some of the people who usually hung around the place. Frankie was impressed that there were even more people wanting to meet him. So with that in mind Frankie, Steve and I headed over to O'Farrell and Jones Streets, the location of the shop.

Steve Monzo, Frankie and the author, on the set of *The Worst of Hollywood*.

Dan understood my explicit instructions for the weekend. No Drinking. None at all. The drinking binges at The Cinema Shop were legendary, but we could have none of it this weekend. "Keep Frankie sober" were the words of the day. I made it clear to all involved that with a sober Frankie all would go well. Upon his arrival at the shop, Frankie was treated like a hero. Dan, who had an encyclopedic knowledge of film, was well versed in Frankie's career, as were the other buffs who had heard through the grapevine that Frankie was coming to town. Dan pulled out the posters and lobby cards from Frankie's films that he had stuffed away in his archives to show Frankie. Frankie loved the attention, gladly answering all the questions that came his way and also posing for photos. As the day wore on, The Cinema Shop swelled with even more fans, each eager to meet their favorite cinema jockey.

Then disaster struck. Some fellow who owned a small market across the street brought in two paper sacks stuffed with six packs of beer and potato chips. "I gotta have a drink with my pal Frankie," he bellowed. It turned out he was a long time Frankie Darro fan and actually knew a lot about his films. Frankie and the group gladly downed one brew, which led to another and then another. I pleaded with Dan to stop the party, but the floodgates had been opened. Once the beers were finished, the market owner returned to his store to replenish the supply after a half hour or so. Someone else opened a bottle of Old Crow, and soon shots were being downed in Frankie's honor. It was quickly out of control. At least it was really early. Steve and I figured that if we got Frankie out soon, he would be able to sleep it off. I convinced him it was time to go back to the hotel, and he agreed.

Frankie was drunk, plain and simple, drunk bad. We'd seen Frankie drink before, but nothing like this. Steve and I each took an arm and led Frankie back to my 1968 Ford Falcon. We slid him in the front passenger side and he kind of just slumped over without talking. Steve sat in the back as I drove silently back to the hotel. It was a very quiet drive until we hit a red light at a busy intersection. Frankie suddenly sprang to life. He rolled down the window, stuck his head out and then shouted for all the world to hear, "It's five o'clock. All Jews off the street. It's five o'clock, get all the Jews off the street!" Steve sprang into action and pulled Frankie back inside and into his seat. Steve explained to Frankie that he shouldn't yell out the window while I raced the final few blocks to the hotel. In defense of Frankie, that was the one and only time we heard him utter an anti-Semitic remark. We brought him back to his room and told Dorothy we would be back the following day at 8 a.m. with a full day's work for Frankie. I figured they would have something to eat then just go to bed.

We had no idea what shape Frankie would be in as we drove back to the hotel the next morning. We hoped for the best. If Frankie could pull this off, he would have a regular job and Steve and I would be involved in some aspect to the show. Everyone could be a winner.

However, when Frankie opened up his hotel room door the next morning, we quickly realized that the sleep, if indeed he got any, did him little good. He was almost as drunk as he had been the night before. He was playful and joking around, but the effects of alcohol were still with him. It was about a half an hour drive from the hotel in downtown to the studio in South San Francisco. We stopped at a gas station and purchased Frankie the largest cup of coffee they had. We kept telling him to drink it up, but he barely touched it. It turned out that he didn't like coffee! Not that it would have done much good, but we thought it might help a bit. Once inside the studio it was quite obvious to all involved that Frankie was still suffering the effects from the previous day's partying. Frankie said he had gone right to bed, but we thought he probably went out drinking with Dorothy. We had given him some spending money upon his arrival so cash was not a problem for the moment.

It was immediately apparent to Steve and me that this was going to be a disaster, and we were correct. They shot the interview portion of the program first. It didn't go very well. Frankie tried hard. He was a veteran trooper after all, but he wasn't very coherent. At one point after being questioned about one of his films, Frankie looked off camera, pointed toward me and proclaimed, "Why don't you ask John, he's over there and he knows all about me." Luckily this wasn't live, it was shot on videotape. We took him outside for a while, tried to ply him with more coffee, but to little avail. They finished shooting a sequence with Frankie hosting the show. They even brought me on to help, but it was useless. Dan called an end to the taping. We said our goodbyes and put Frankie back into the car. All hopes for his new TV career had ended with a crash. So had Steve and mine actually.

As fate would have it, a few months later Dan booked Mantan Moreland as a guest. Mantan was great, funny and sharp. His ability did not go unnoticed. The station manager enjoyed Mantan so much that he hired him to host a show on Saturday nights. They flew him up once a week for his hosting duties then flew him back to Los Angeles. Often Steve and I would either pick him up from the airport or deliver him back. It was an honor to spend time in his presence. At least someone got a job after all this.

Frankie called me a few weeks after his return and thanked all of us for the wonderful time he had had. He said he'd love to do it again and that next time he would do it without salary. Just pay his expenses and he would be there. As far as Frankie was concerned all had gone well that day!

Four months later Steve and I were back in Hollywood sitting in Frankie's apartment. He had moved, temporarily as it turned out, to the Rector Hotel, a few blocks east of the St. Francis. The room looked the same. We didn't ask the reason of the move, but I did ask if he had brought the box of memorabilia with him. "Oh yes, that follows me everywhere," he mused. He got up from his chair, went to a small closet that was almost empty except for the box, and set the box in front of me for my perusal. He must have realized my total fascination with its contents, for without hesitation and in an off handed way he said, "John, you like this stuff so much, why don't you just take it?" Shocked, I replied "No, Frankie, this box is all you have left from your career. All your memories are here, I can't take it. However, if the time comes that you really need some cash, call me and I'll buy it from you." He agreed.

While walking back to the car, Steve called me a fool for not taking the box. We would have many conversations about the box over the years, and it always came down to me being a fool for not taking it that day. And now I would have to say, "Steve you were correct!"

Unfortunately Mantan's didn't host his show very long. As the weeks went by, his health, which hadn't been good for some time, began to fail seriously. He became weaker and weaker, and eventually he had to give up the show. He died on September 28, 1973. Frankie was an honorary pall bearer. After the funeral Frankie stated how important Mantan was to his career. "Yeah, Mantan was unique among humanity, all right-and a great a pal as he was an artist".

Amazingly, Frankie would work again. In 1974 he was hired for a one day bit in the TV movie *The Girl On the Late Late Show.* It featured other old timers such as Yvonne DeCarlo, Gloria Graham, and Walter Pidgeon. Frankie showed up for about twenty seconds as a studio guard. Shown mostly in shadows viewers would miss him except for his distinctive voice. First telecast on April 1, 1974 it was designed as a pilot for a series to star Don Murray, but the show did not sell. Frankie's final appearance in front of the camera was in the feature *Fugitive Lovers.* Filmed under the title *Star Crash*, it was another payday for old timers like Virginia Mayo and Doddles Weaver. Frankie plays Lester the town drunk, seen in a sequence that lasts for only a few seconds. He's sitting in a jail holding cell, dressed in his personal clothes, flailing his arms about and talking almost incoherently. Unfortunately it's difficult to say if he was really acting or not because he looks to be really drunk. After shooting his brief scene, the director John Carr went over to Frankie and congratulated him on his performance. "I've had years of practice," Frankie responded. Frankie had to "sic" the Screen Actors Guild on the company for not paying him. It's not known in fact if he was ever paid. The film was supposedly released in 1975. All of Frankie's fans should avoid the film.

After *The Worst of Hollywood* debacle, both Steve and I were disappointed with the outcome, of course, but our frequent visits with Frankie continued unabated. When we did visit we would usually plan to show up in the late morning because if we showed up later in the day, Frankie would have already started to drink. The strange thing was that as much alcohol as Frankie consumed, he was never a bad drunk per se. Sure, he'd get sloppy in his speech and all, but he would never become belligerent or mean spirited. Diana Serra Cary, the former child star know as Baby Peggy, called Frankie one evening. She was doing research for her indispensable book "Hollywood's Children." Her former crush was so drunk that he was almost completely unintelligible. One strange fact about Frankie was that he would rail against illegal drugs. To Frankie's thinking people who took illegal drugs were bums, plain and simple. He had no tolerance for anyone who used illegal drugs.

As it happened, we did see him lose his temper, but only once, early on in our visits, on September 5, 1972. We had just arrived from our five hour trip from the Bay Area to find Frankie sitting in front of the television screaming, "God damm A-rabs!" along with other choice epithets. Arab terrorists had taken Israeli athletes hostage at the Olympics and eventually killed 17 of them. Frankie was watching the whole event unfold before him. Steve and I had not yet heard the news. We had played our collection of movie soundtracks during the trip.

Once we showed up at the St. Francis, but Frankie was not home. We got back in the car and were driving down Hollywood Boulevard when we saw some guy jaywalking. Steve slammed on the brakes so as not to run him over, and it turned out to be Frankie making a quick run to the liquor store. Frankie climbed into the car, and we took him to lunch, then back to his hotel. For some reason we never called him to warn him that we were in town. We just showed up, and he never seemed to mind.

Frankie never went to the movies. It had been years since he'd been inside a movie theater, even though Hollywood Boulevard was dotted with them at the time. He did love his TV, however. Late one night he was watching an interview show, and the guest was none other than William Wellman. The host asked Wild Bill who is favorite actor was, out of all the ones he had worked with. With names like Gable, Cooper, and Mitchum to choose from, he thought for a minute and stated, "Frankie Darro." He then added, "There was only one thing wrong with Frankie...he never grew taller. He couldn't play adult roles at his size." The fact that Wellman acknowledged him in this way was very meaningful to Frankie.

Since *The Worst of Hollywood* didn't work out as Steve and I had hoped, we came up with another idea. I owned a 16 MM motion picture camera. A few years earlier we had filmed our version of the 1945 Republic serial *The Purple Monster Strikes*. Steve portrayed the Purple Monster, and in our version he really was purple. Anyway, we had the idea of making another movie, only this time it was to star Frankie. We ran the idea by him, and he was all for it. His only stipulation was that it had to be filmed at the hotel. The plot was something about murders at a hotel, with Frankie playing an out of work jockey. Unfortunately the idea didn't go much beyond an outline and a few shots of the exterior of the St. Francis. Frankie would ask us about the project on occasion, until the idea was dropped altogether.

During one of our visits, I had brought a scrapbook I had been putting together. It was filled with stills, clippings and whatever else I could find on Frankie. I was proud of what I had been able to put together. When I had presented it to Frankie, he seemed interested but quickly put it down and began talking of something else. Later I was elected to make a food run. It was to be a quick trip to Kentucky Fried Chicken to pick up a meal for the three of us. Later that night, on our way back to Steve's aunt's house, he was chomping at the bit to tell me something. It turns out that when I had left to get the food, Frankie had voiced his concern to Steve about me. Frankie thought it was strange that I would bother putting together a scrapbook on his career. He was worried that I might have a problem of some sort. Steve assured Frankie that as far as he knew, I was normal and Frankie shouldn't worry, that I also had scrapbooks on Laurel and Hardy, The Marx Brothers and all sorts of other actors from the golden age of Hollywood. It pleased Frankie to hear that, and the subject was dropped.

Frankie's life seemed to run in pretty much of a rut. After shaking off the previous night's hangover, he would drink orange juice or lemonade. He never seemed to eat much, but by noon or so he was out looking for a drink. On occasion when we would bring food or drinks over (never liquor by the way), he would tell us, "Boys, you should have known me when I had money. Life was great and I would have paid for everything." It never bothered us that he was broke. He was our friend; that was all that mattered. Realizing his dire financial situation I once suggested to him that he might be able to find a job at one of the stores dotting Hollywood Boulevard. "John, acting is all I know how to do," he responded. He mentioned that early on he had wanted to become a director, and that once at Monogram one of the directors let him direct a scene in one of his movies. He had really enjoyed the experience but nothing ever came of this desire.

When he needed a health check up or some dental work done, he'd go over to The Motion Picture Hospital in Calabasas. Almost everyone in show business pays a percentage of their paycheck to the hospital. Then in return they can obtain free health care. It was a blessing for someone in Frankie's position. During the hot summer days when it never seemed as if it would ever cool down, the symptoms of Frankie's malaria would return. Drinking helped because at least he would be numb to the effects, but the symptoms would always return the following day.

Hollywood had forgotten about Frankie, but some of his fans had not. His daily mail brought a smattering of fan mail and an occasional residual check. When fans would ask detailed questions, he would often give them my address or phone number. More than just a few times my phone would ring at an odd hour with someone wanting to know something about Frankie. One of Frankie's fans wrote to me saying he was glad I was writing the story of Frankie's life. That was in 1974. Frankie asked me to put together a list of his film credits, something he could mail to fans. In the days before books on movies lined shelves at bookstores, this was a difficult task. I compiled a list from the few reference works available and presented it to Frankie. "John, I made a lot more movies than this," he said shaking his head. When I asked him for additional titles he could never come up with any. I worked on the list off and on, and he would request copies frequently. In May 1974 the Royal Theater on Santa Monica Boulevard in Los Angeles held a William Wellman film festival. Wellman himself was present for a showing of *Wild Boys of the Road.* The film was well reviewed by Kevin Thomas in the Los Angeles Times. Writing about Frankie, Thomas noted, "The performers are most engaging with Darro outstanding in his Cagney-like feistiness and grace." Frankie might have read this contemporary review, but he was not at the screening.

On Sunday April 11, 1976 Frankie's father Frankie Darro, Sr. died at a convalescent hospital in Hollywood. He had seen his talented son's rise in the ranks of movie stardom, just as he had hoped for. But he also lived long enough to see his son's crash to the bottom. Darro Sr. had also lived at the St. Francis for years, like his son. He was eighty-eight years old when he died.

During the summer of 1976, the Pacific Film Archive, located on the campus at the University of California in Berkeley, hosted a tribute to William Wellman. Wellman had passed away the previous year. Included in the tribute was a showing of *Wild Boys of the Road*, I jumped at the chance to finally see the film Frankie spoke so highly of. The archive only held about fifty people, and less than half the seats were filled. As the film unspooled I sat there mesmerized. There he was, Frankie in all his glory – funny, sad, but most of all full of energy, just about knocking everyone else off the screen, but not stealing scenes as some actors are known to do. On the drive home I realized what Frankie was capable of. This was a star making role. The next day I called Frankie to tell him what I thought of the film. He was very happy that I'd finally seen it. "You were great Frankie," I told him. He replied, "Yeah, maybe so. That was one of the good ones." He gave William Wellman all the credit for the film's success.

In early January 1977 I went to my mailbox and pulled out a copy of "Daily Variety", along with the rest of my mail. As I walked back to my apartment, I glanced through the issue and in the back spotted Frankie's obituary. It ran only two short paragraphs, not nearly long enough for someone whose whole life was spent in show business. On Christmas Day 1976 Frankie and Dorothy were visiting her daughter (from a previous marriage) in Huntington Beach, about a forty-five minute drive from Hollywood. Upon their arrival Frankie had complained of not feeling well and went into a bedroom to lie down. When his wife came to call him for dinner, she couldn't waken him. An ambulance was called, and he was taken to Huntington Intercommunity Hospital. He died in the hospital that night at 9:01 of a heart attack brought on by cardiovascular disease. He had turned fifty-nine just a few weeks before. His body was cremated on December 29, and his ashes were scattered in the ocean off Long Beach.

Among my first thoughts when I read about Frankie's passing was a concern for his box of memorabilia. It should be saved. Not necessarily for me, but perhaps in a library somewhere. Would Dorothy toss it in a dumpster? I toyed with the idea of visiting her on one of our trips to L.A., but we never did. I'm positive we would not have been welcome. The memories of Frankie, his friendship, his eternal optimism and the box stayed with me for years.

CHAPTER 19
EPILOGUE

Frankie's passing made so little news that on March 8, 1977, a local newspaper stated in their celebrity questions column that Frankie was still alive. Darlene, long estranged from her father, would not learn of his passing until 1980.

In June 1981 Frankie made the front page of the newspaper *Los Angeles Globe*. The article featured a large picture of Frankie, along with another of actress Gloria Jean, with a headline that read "Stars Without Stars." The article written by Hal Smith bemoaned the fact that Frankie, long with hundreds of other actors, did not have stars on the celebrated Walk of Fame along Hollywood Boulevard. Smith knew Frankie's father and was very complimentary toward Frankie. As of this writing he still does not have a star. With the price of the star now at $15,000, it's doubtful he'll ever have one.

After Frankie's passing Dorothy continued to work at the clothing store on Hollywood Boulevard. She died on July 9, 1984.

In 1992, just a few weeks shy of his fortieth birthday, my friend Steve Monzo passed away after a lengthy illness. We talked about Frankie often during the final days. "You should have taken the box!" was his frequent comment during those visits.

Frankie's daughter moved to Oregon a few years ago after living most of her life in the Long Beach, California area. She recently celebrated her sixty-third birthday.

In 2005, items from Frankie's memorabilia collection started showing up on eBay. Some of the autographed photos fetched well over $100 each. It turned out that Frankie eventually sold some of the contents of the box to someone else.

Frankie wouldn't recognize Hollywood today. It's been scrubbed clean and redeveloped to be almost unrecognizable. The boulevard is spotted with trendy night clubs and restaurants. The hookers have long since moved south of Santa Monica Boulevard. The St. Francis Hotel is currently undergoing a refurbishing. It looks better today than it probably ever did, even in its heyday.

Frankie's bar Try Later is long gone; in its place is the tony O-Bar. It's safe to say that the celebrities drinking and dining in its beautiful surroundings have never heard the name Frankie Darro.

FBO, the first studio to place Frankie under contract, is a long forgotten entity. However, one artifact remains. On the Paramount lot in Hollywood there is one manhole cover with the initials, FBO, a quiet reminder of another era. Monogram Studios is another long forgotten entity, but the old studio still stands. Today it's the home of KCET, a public broadcasting station.

With the advent of home video in the 1980's, films of all eras suddenly became much more accessible. When the DVD boom hit in the mid 1990's, it became even easier to obtain B films from the 30's and 40's at "sell through" prices. Frankie's films from the Mascot, Conn and Monogram days started to appear on store shelves everywhere. Frankie would not have minded that Mantan now receives top billing. At least the films are available. The popular cable channel TCM keeps *Wild Boys of the Road* alive, playing it constantly, along with Frankie's other early Warner Bros. films.

Now, with the easy access to many of his films, they can finally be reappraised for the little gems they are. With Frankie's energy, spunkiness and charm, viewers can sit back and still be entertained by him after all these many years.

ACKNOWLEDGMENTS

First off, a big thanks to Frankie Darro himself for befriending a couple of teenagers so many years ago. Sorry Frankie that it took so many years to tell your story.

Another big thanks to the following for sharing their memories of working with Frankie: The late William Benedict, Virginia Davis, the late Marcia Mae Jones, Adrian Booth Brian, the late Mantan Moreland, Frank Coughlin, Jr., Dorothy Coonan Wellman, Dick Jones, Noel Neill, Richard Anderson and Anne Francis.

Without the invaluable help of Diana Serra Cary the stories of Frankie's early years would have been lost to the ages.

A special thank you to William Wellman, Jr. for being so willing to answer my questions, and always in a warm humorous way.

Thanks also go to Henry Park, Mark Pitta, Bob Shaw, Geela, John and Marge Stringer, Les Hammer, Michael von-Baron, Steve Beasley, Victor Quevedo, Nina Anderson, Mike Rounds and of course Darlene Darro-Hollis, Frankie's daughter.

A very special thank you to Paul and Marie Picerni for their friendship and encouragement.

The following organizations were most helpful, especially Donovan Brandt at Eddie Brandts' Saturday Matinee, not only the best video store on the planet but the friendliest!

The staff of The Margaret Herrick Library at The Academy of Motion Picture Arts and Sciences, especially Russ Butner. The Glendale Library and the Los Angeles Central Library. UCLA Film and Television Archives (Mark Gens). The American Film Institute, their on-line catalog contains story information on many of Frankie's lost silent films.

Another special thank you to Emily S. Carmen, Curator at the Warner Bros. Archives at U.S.C. School of Cinematic Arts, Ms. Carmen unearthed a treasure trove of material from Frankie's years at Warner Bros.

Web sites: paper-dragon.com, imdb.com, variety.com, kirjasto. sci.fi.com, wikipedia.org., afi.com, oscars.org, warnerbros.com, Accurance.com (Special Thanks to William B. Earle), and ebay.com.
And of course, Bea.

FILMOGRAPHY

JUDGMENT OF THE STORM (1924)
A Palmer Production D: Del Andrews
CAST: Claire McDowell, Lucile Rickson, George Hackathorne,
Frankie Darro (Heath Twin).

RACING FOR LIFE (1924)
Columbia Pictures D: Henry MacRae
CAST: Eva Novak, William Fairbanks, Philo McCullough, Frankie
Darro (Jimmy Danton).

SIGNAL TOWER (1924)
Universal D: Clarence L. Brown
CAST: Virginia Valli, Rickliffe Fellowes, Frankie Darro (Sonny
Taylor), Wallace Berry.

ROARING RAILS (1924)
Producers Distributing Corp. A Hunt Stromberg Production D: Tom
Forman
CAST: Harry Carey, Edith Roberts, Wallace MacDonald, Frankie
Darro (Little Bill).

HALF-A-DOLLAR-BILL (1924)
Metro D: William S. Van Dyke
CAST: Anna Q. Nilsson, William P. Carleton, Raymond Hatton,
Frankie Darro (Half-A-Dollar-Bill).

WOMEN AND GOLD (1925)
Lumis Film Corp. D: James P. Hogan
CAST: Frank Mayo, Sylvia Breamer, William Davidson, Frankie
Darrow (Dan Barclay, Jr.).

LET'S GO GALLAGHER (1925)
FBO D: Robert DeLacy

CAST: Tom Tyler, Barbara Starr, Olin Francis, Frankie Darro (Little Joey).

THE MIDNIGHT FLYER (1925)
FBO D: Tom Forman
CAST: Cullen Landis, Dorothy Devore, Buddy Post, Frankie Darro (Young Davey).

THE FEARLESS LOVER (1925)
Perfection Pictures D: Henry MacRae
CAST: William Fairbanks, Eva Novak, Tom Kennedy, Frankie Darrow (Frankie).

THE COWBOY MUSKETEER (1925)
FBO D: Robert DeLacy
CAST: Tom Tyler, Jim London, Frances Dare, Frankie Darro (Billy).

FIGHTING THE FLAMES (1925)
Columbia Pictures D: Reeves Eason
CAST: William Haines, Dorothy Devore, Frankie Darro (Mickey).

THE WYOMING WILDCAT (1925)
FBO D: Robert DeLacy
CAST: Tom Tyler, Billie Bennett, G. Clayton, Frankie Darro (Barney Finn).

THE PHANTOM EXPRESS (1925)
Banner Productions D: John Adolfi
CAST: Ethel Shannon, George Periolat, David Butler, Frankie Darro (Daddles).

WANDERING FOOTSTEPS (1925)
Banner Productions D: Phil Rosen
CAST: Alec B. Francis, Estelle Taylor, Bryant Washburn, Frankie Darro (Billy).

PEOPLE VERSUS NANCY PRESTON (1925)
Producers Distributing Corp. D: Tom Forman CAST: Marguerite
DeLaMotte, John Bowers, Frankie Darro (Bubsy).

CONFESSIONS OF A QUEEN (1925)
Metro-Goldwyn D: Victor Seastrom
CAST: Alice Terry, Lewis Stone, John Bowers, Frankie Darro (Prince
Zara).

BUSTIN' THROUGH (1925)
Universal D: Clifford Smith
CAST: Jack Hoxie, Helen Lynch, Frankie Darro. Frankie's appearence
has not been confirmed.

SO BIG (1924)
First National D: Charles Brabin
CAST: Colleen Moore, Joseph De Grasse, John Bowers, Frankie
Darrow (Dirk as a boy).

FLAMING WATERS
Metro-Goldwyn D: Marshall Neilan
CAST: Sally O'Neill, William Haines, Charles Murray, Frankie Darro
(A Boy).

HEARTS AND SPANGLES (1926)
Lumas Pictures Corp. D: Frank O'Connor
CAST: George Chesbro, Charles Force, Robert Gordon, Frankie
Darrow (Bobby).

MEMORY LANE (1926)
First National D: John M. Stahl
CAST: Eleanor Broadman, Conrad Nagel, William Haines, Frankie
Darro (Urchin).

HER HUSBANDS SECRET (1925)
First National Pictures D: Frank Lloyd

CAST: Antonio Moreno, Patsy Ruth Miller,
Frankie Darro (Young Elliot Miller).

KIKI (1926)
First National D: Clarence Brown
CAST: Ronald Coleman, Gertrude Astor,
Frankie Darro (Pierre).

TOM AND HIS PALS (1926)
FBO D: Robert DeLacy
CAST: Tom Tyler, Doris Hill, Dicky Brandon,
Frankie Darro (Frankie Smith).

WILD TO GO (1926)
FBO D: Robert DeLacy
CAST: Tom Tyler, Frankie Darrow (Frankie Blake), Fred Burns,
Ethan Laidlaw.

THE COWBOY COP (1926)
FBO D: Robert DeLacy
CAST: Tom Tyler, Jean Arthur, Irvin Renard,
Frankie Darro (Frankie).

THE CARNIVAL GIRL (1926)
Assc. Exhibitors D: Cullen Tate
CAST: Marion Mack, Gladys Brockwell, George
Siegmann, Frankie Darro (Mack's brother).

RED HOT HOOFS (1926)
FBO D: Robert DeLacy
CAST: Tom Tyler, Dorothy Dunbal, Stanley
Taylor, Frankie Darro (Frankie Buckley).

BORN TO BATTLE (1926)
FBO D: Robert DeLacy
Tom Tyler, Jean Arthur, Ray Childs, Frankie
Darro (Birdie).

OUT OF THE WEST (1926)
FBO D: Robert DeLacy
CAST: Tom Tyler, Bernice Welch, L.J. O'Connor,
Frankie Darro (Frankie).

THE MASQUERADE BANDIT (1926)
FBO D: Robert DeLacy
Tom Tyler, Dorothy Dunbar, Ethan Laidlaw,
Frankie Darro (Tim Marble).

THE THRILL HUNTERS (1926)
Columbia D: Eugene De Rue CAST: William Hainnes, Kathryn
McGuire, Frankie Darro (Boy Prince).

THE ARIZONA STREAK (1926)
FBO D: Robert DeLacy
CAST: Tom Tyler, Alfred Hewston, Ada Mae
Vaughn, Frankie Darro (Mike).

MIKE (1926)
Metro-Goldwyn D: Marshall Neilan
CAST: Salley O"Neal, William Haines, Charles
Murray, Frankie Darro (Boy).

LIGHTING LARIATS (1927)
FBO D: Robert DeLacy
CAST: Tom Tyler, Dorothy Dunbar, Rudy Blaine,
Frankie Darro (Alexis, King of Roxenburg).

HER FATHER SAID NO (1927)
FBO D: Jack McKeown
CAST: Mary Brian, Danny O'Shea, Al Cooke,
Frankie Darro (Matt Doe).

FLYING U RANCH (1927)
FBO D: Robert DeLacy

CAST: Tom Tyler, Nora Lane, Barney Furey,
Frankie Darro (Chip, Jr.).

FLESH AND THE DEVIL (1927)
MGM D: Clarence Brown
CAST: John Gilbert, Greta Garbo,
Lars Hanson, Frankie Darro (Party Guest).

JUDGMENT OF THE HILLS (1927)
FBO D: James Leo Meehan
CAST: Virginia Valli, Orville Caldwell, Frankie
Darro (Ted Dennison).

MOULDERS OF MEN (1927)
FBO D: Ralph Ince
CAST : Conway Tearle, Margaret Morris, Frankie
Darro (Sandy Barry), Rex Lease.

TOM'S GANG (1927)
FBO D: Robert DeLacy
CAST: Tom Tyler, Sharon Lynn, Frankie Darro
(Spuds).

LONG PANTS (1927)
First National Pictures D: Frank Capra CAST: Harry Langdon,
Gladys, Brodwell.
Frankie Darro played Langdon's character as a
small child. The part was cut from the final release
print.

CYCLONE OF THE RANGE (1927)
FBO D: Robert DeLacy
CAST: Tom Tyler, Elsie Tarron, Harry O'Connor,
Frankie Darro (Frankie Butler).

LITTLE MICKEY GROGAN (1927)
FBO D:Leo Meehan

CAST: Frankie Darrow (Grogan), Jobyna Ralston, Crawford Kent.

THE DESERT PIRATE (1927)
FBO D: James Dugan
CAST: Tom Tyler, Duane Thompson, Edward Hearne, Frankie Darro (Jimmy Rand).

WHEN THE LAW RIDES (1928)
FBO D: Robert DeLacy
CAST: Tom Tyler, Jane Reid, Frankie Darro (Frankie Ross), Joshua Thurston.

THE TEXAS TORNADO (1928)
FBO D: Frank Howard Clark
CAST: Tom Tyler, Frankie Darro (Bud Martin,) Nora Lane, Jack Anthony.

TYRANT OF RED GULCH (1928)
FBO D: Robert DeLacy
CAST: Tom Tyler, Frankie Darro ("Tip"), Barney Furey, Harry Woods.

TERROR MOUNTAIN (1928)
FBO D: Louis King
CAST: Tom Tyler, Jane Reid, Al Ferguson, Frankie Darro (Buddy Roberts).

PHANTOM OF THE RANGE (1928)
FBO D: James Dugan
CAST: Tom Tyler, Duan Thompson, Charles McHugh, Frankie Darro (Spuds O'Brien).

THE CIRCUS KID (1928)
FBO D: George B. Seitz
CAST: Frankie Darro (Buddy,) Joe E. Brown, Poodles Hanneford, Helene Costello.

THE AVENGING RIDER (1928)
FBO D: Wallace Fox
CAST: Tom Tyler, Florence Allen, Frankie Darro
(Frankie Sheridan), Al Ferguson.

TRAIL OF THE HORSE THIEVES (1929)
FBO D: Robert DeLacy
CAST: Tom Tyler, Sharon Lynn, Frankie Darro
(Buddy).

IDAHO RED (1929)
FBO D: Robert DeLacy
CAST: Tom Tyler, Patricia Caron, Frankie Darro
(Tadpole), Lew Meehan.

PRIDE OF THE PAWNEE (1929)
FBO D: Robert DeLacy
CAST: Tom Tyler, Ethlyne Claire, Barney Furey,
Frankie Darro (Jerry Wilson).

GUN LAW (1929)
FBO D: Robert DeLacy and John Burch
CAST: Tom Tyler, Barney Furey, Ethlyn Claire,
Frankie Darro (Buster Brown).

RAINBOW MAN (1929)
Sono-Art D: Fred Newmeyer
CAST: Eddie Dowling, Frankie Darrow (Billy Ryan),
Marian Nixon, Sam Hardy.

BLAZE O' GLORY (1930)
Sono-Art D: Renaud Hoffman
CAST: Eddie Dowling, Betty Compson, Frankie
Darro (Gene Williams), Ferdinand Schummann-
Heink.

THREE ON A MATCH (1931)
Warner Bros. D: Mervyn LeRoy
CAST: Joan Blondell, Warren Williams, Ann Dvorak, Humphrey
Bogart, Frankie Darro (Bobby).

LIGHTNING WARRIOR (1931)
Mascot (Serial) D: Armand Schaefer and Ben Kline
CAST: Rin Tin Tin, Frankie Darro (Jimmy Carter),
Georgia Hale, George Brent.

PUBLIC ENEMY (1931)
Warner Bros. D: William A. Wellman CAST: James Cagney, Jean
Harlow, Edward Woods, Joan Blondell, Frankie Darro (Matt as a boy).

SIN OF MADELON CLAUDET (1931)
MGM D: Edgar Selwyn
CAST: Helen Hayes, Lewis Stone, Neil Hamilton,
Frankie Darro (Larry at age 12).

MAD GENIUS (1931)
Warner Bros. D: Michael Curtiz
CAST: John Barrymore, Marian Marsh, Donald
Cook, Boris Karloff, Frankie Darro (Fedor as a boy).

VANISHING LEGION (1931)
Mascot-Serial D: B. Reeves Eason
CAST: Harry Carey, Edwina Booth, Rex the horse, Philo McCullough,
Frankie Darro (Jimmy
Williams), Joe Bonomo.

AMATEUR DADDY (1932)
Fox D: John G. Blystone
CAST: Warner Baxter, Marian Nixon, Rita LaRoy,
Frankie Darro (Pete Smith).

WAY BACK HOME (1931)
RKO D: William Seiter

CAST: Phillips H. Lord, Effie Palmer, Bette Davis, Frankie Darro (Robbie).

THE CHEYENNE CYCLONE (1932)
Willis Kent Prod. D: Armand Schaeffer
CAST: Lane Chandler, Connie LaMont, Frankie Darro ('Orphan' McGuire), Yakima Canutt.

THE DEVIL HORSE (1932)
Mascot-Serial D: Otto Brower
CAST: Harry Carey, Noah Beery, Frankie Darro (wild boy), Apache the horse.

THE WOLF DOG (1933)
Mascot-Serial D: Harry Frazer and Colbert Clark
CAST: Frankie Darro (Frank), Rin Tin Tin, Jr., George Lewis, Boots Mallory, Henry B. Walthall.

THE MAYOR OF HELL (1933)
Warner Bros. D: Archie Mayo
Cast: James Cagney, Madge Evans, Allen Jenkins, Dudley Digges, Frankie Darro (Jimmy).

WILD BOYS OF THE ROAD (1933)
Warner Bros. D: William A. Wellman
CAST: Frankie Darro (Eddie Smith), Dorothy Coonan, Rochelle Hudson, Edwin Phillips, Ann Hovey, Arthur Hohl, Grant Mitchell.

TUGBOAT ANNIE (1933)
MGM D: Mervyn LeRoy
CAST: Marie Dressler, Wallace Beery, Robert Young, Maureen O'Sullivan, Frankie Darro (Alec as a child).

LAUGHING AT LIFE (1933)
Mascot D: Ford Beebe

CAST: Victor McLaughlin, Conchita Montenegro, William Boyd, Frankie Darro (Chango).

BIG RACE (1933)
Showmen's Pictures D: Fred Newmeyer
CAST: Boots Mallory, John Darrow, Paul Hurst, Frankie Darro (Jockey).

THE MERRY FRINKS (1934)
Warner Bros. D: Alfred E. Green
CAST: Aline MacMahon, Guy Kibbee, Hugh Herbert, Allen Jenkins, Frankie Darro (Norman).

BROADWAY BILL (1934)
Columbia Pictures D: Frank Capra
CAST: Warner Baxter, Myrna Loy, Walter Connolly, Jason Robards Sr., Frankie Darro (Ted Williams).

NO GREATER GLORY (1934)
Columbia Pictures D: Frank Borzage
CAST: George Breakston, Frankie Darro (Feri Afs), Jimmy Butler, Jackie Searl.

BURN 'EM UP BARNES (1934)
Mascot-Serial D: Colbert Clark and Armand Schaefer
CAST: Jack Mulhall, Frankie Darro (Bobby), Lola Lane, Julian Rivero, Edwin Maxwell.

LITTLE MEN (1934)
Mascot D: Phil Rosen
CAST: Ralph Morgan, Erin O'Brien-Moore, Junior Durkin, Cora Sue Collins, Phyllis Fraser, Frankie Darro (Dan), David Doran, Dickie Moore.

MEN OF ACTION (1935)
Conn Pictures D: Alan James
CAST: Frankie Darro (Jimmy Morgan), Roy Mason, Syd Saylor.

VALLEY OF WANTED MEN (1935)
Conn Pictures D: Alan James
CAST: Frankie Darro ('Slivers' Sanderson), Roy Mason Russell
Hopton, Grant Withers.

STRANDED (1935)
Warners Bros. D: Frank Borzage
CAST: Kay Francis, George Brent, Patricia Ellis, Donald Woods,
Frankie Darro (Jimmy Rivers).

THE PAYOFF (1935)
Warner Bros. D: Robert Florey
CAST: James Dunn, Claire Dodd, Patricia Ellis, Allan Dinehart,
Joseph Crehan, Frankie Darro (Jimmy Moore), Frank Sheridan.

RED HOT TIRES (1935)
Warner Bros. D: Ross Ledermann
CAST: Lyle Talbot, Mary Astor, Roscoe Karns, Frankie Darro
(Johnny), Gavin Gordon.

THE PHANTOM EMPIRE (1935)
Mascot-Serial D: Otto Brewer and B. Reeves
Eason
CAST: Gene Autry, Frankie Darro (Frankie), Betsy
Ross King, Dorothy Christy, Wheeler Oakman.

THE EX-MRS. BRADFORD (1936)
RKO D: Stephen Roberts
CAST: William Powell, Jean Arthur, James Gleason, Frankie Darro
(Spike Salsbury).

CHARLIE CHAN AT THE RACE TRACK (1936)
20th Century Fox D: H. Bruce Humberstone
CAST: Warner Oland, Keye Luke, Helen Wood, Thomas Beck, Frank
Coghlan, Jr., Frankie Darro ('Tip' Collins).

RACING BLOOD (1936)
Conn Pictures D: Rex Hale
CAST: Frankie Darro (Frankie Reynolds), Kane Richmond, Gladys
Blake, Arthur Houseman.

DEVIL DIAMOND (1937)
Conn Pictures D: Les Goodwins
CAST: Frankie Darro (Lee), Kane Richmond, June Gale, Rosita
Butler.

SARATOGA (1937)
MGM D: Jack Conway
CAST: Clark Gable, Jean Harlow, Lionel Barrymore, Frankie Darro
(Dixie Gordon).

THOROUGHBREDS DON'T CRY (1937)
MGM D: Alfred E. Green
CAST: Judy Garland, Mickey Rooney, Ronald Sinclair, Sophie
Tucker, C. Aubrey Smith, Frankie Darro ('Dink' Reid), Henry Kolker.

MIND YOUR OWN BUSINESS (1936)
Paramount D: Norman McLeod
CAST: Charlie Ruggles, Alice Brady, Lyle Talbot, Frankie Darro
(Bob).

BORN TO FIGHT (1936)
Conn Pictures D: Les Goodwins
CAST: Frankie Darro ('Baby Face' Madison), Kane Richmond, Jack
LaRue, Frances Grant, Sheila Mannors.

ANYTHING FOR A THRILL (1937)
Conn Pictures D: Les Goodwins
CAST: Frankie Darro (Dan Mallory), Kane Richmond, June Johnson,
Ann Evers, Johnston White, Horace Murphy, Eddie Hearn.

YOUNG DYNAMITE (1937)
Conn Pictures D: Les Goodwins

CAST: Frankie Darro (Freddie), Kane Richmond,
Charlotte Henry, David Sharpe, William Costello, Carlton Young, Pat
Gleason.

HEADLINE CRASHER (1937)
Conn Pictures D: Les Goodwins
CAST: Frankie Darro (Jimmy Tallant), Kane Richmond, Muriel
Evans, John Merton, Richard Tucker, Edward Earle, Eleanor Steward.

A DAY AT THE RACES (1937)
MGM D: Sam Wood
CAST: Groucho, Chico and Harpo Marx, Allen Jones, Maureen
O'Sullivan, Frankie Darro (Morgan's Jockey).

JUVENILE COURT (1938)
Columbia Pictures D: D. Ross Lederman
CAST: Paul Kelly, Rita Hayworth, Hally Chester, Frankie Darro
(Stubby).

REFORMATORY (1938) Columbia Pictures D: Lewis D. Collins
CAST: Jack Holt, Bobby Jordan, Charlotte Wynters, Grant Mitchell,
Tommy Bupp, Frankie Darro (Louie Miller), Ward Bond, Shelia
Bromley.

WANTED BY THE POLICE (1938)
Monogram D: Howard Bretherton
CAST: Frankie Darro (Jerry), Lillian Dlliot, Robert Kent, Evalyn
Knapp, Matti Fain, Don Rowan.

THE GREAT ADVENTURES OF WILD BILL HICKOK (1938)
Columbia Pictures-Serial D: Mack V. Wright and Sam Nelson
CAST: Gordon Elliot, Monte Blue, Carole Wayne, Frankie Darro
(Jerry), Dickie Jones.

TOUGH KID (1938)
Monogram D: Howard Bretherton

CAST: Frankie Darro (Skipper Murphy), Dick Purcell, Judith Allen, Lillian Elliott, Don Rowan.

BOYS REFORMATORY (1939)
Monogram D: Howard Bretherton
CAST: Frankie Darro (Tommy), Grant Withers, Dave Durand, Warren McCollum, Frank Coghlan, Jr., Ben Weldon, Lillian Elliott, Bob McClung.

IRISH LUCK (1939)
Monogram D: Howard Bretherton
CAST: Frankie Darro (Buzzy O'Brien), Dick Purcell, Lillian Elliott, Shelia Darcy, James Flavin, Dennis Moore, Mantan Moreland, Howard Mitchell.

CHASING TROUBLE (1940)
Monogram D: Howard Bretherton
CAST: Frankie Darro (Frankie 'Cupid' O'Brien, Marjorie Reynolds, Mantan Moreland, Milburn Stone, Cheryl Walker, George Cleveland.

MEN WITH STEEL FACES (1940)
Mascot/Times Release
Feature version of the serial THE PHANTOM EMPIRE.

LAUGHING AT DANGER (1940)
Monogram D: Howard Bretherton
CAST: Frankie Darro (Frankie Kelly), Joy Hodges, George Houston, Mantan Moreland, Kay Sutton, Guy Usher, Lillian Elliott, Veda Ann Borg.

ON THE SPOT (1940)
Monogram D: Howard Bretherton
CAST: Frankie Darro (Frankie Kelly), Mary Kornman, Mantan Moreland, John St. Polls, Robert Warwick, Lillian Elliott, Maxine Leslie.

PINOCCHIO (1940)
RKO P: Walt Disney

Voice Talent: Dickie Jones, Cliff Edwards, Christian Rub, Frankie Darro (Lampwick).

UP IN THE AIR (1940)
Monogram D: Howard Bretherton
CAST: Frankie Darro (Frankie Ryan), Marjorie Reynolds, Mantan Moreland, Gordon Jones, Lorna Grey, Tristram Coffin, Clyde Dilson.

THE GANGS ALL HERE (1941)
Monogram D: Jean Yarbrough
CAST: Frankie Darro (Frankie), Marcia Mae Jones, Mantan Moreland, Jackie Moran, Keye Luke, Robert Homans, Irving Mitchell, Ed Cassidy.

YOU'RE OUT OF LUCK (1941)
Monogram D: Howard Bretherton
CAST: Frankie Darro (Frankie O'Reilly), Kay Sutton, Mantan Moreland, Vicki Lester, Richard Bond, Janet Shaw, Tristram Coffin, Ralph Peters.

TUXEDO JUNCTION (1941)
Republic Pictures D: Frank McDonald
CAST: Leon, Frank and June Weaver, Thurston Hall, Frankie Darro ('Sock'), Sally Payne, Clayton Moore, Lorna Grey, Billy Benedict, Ken Lundy.

LET'S GO COLLEGIATE (1941)
Monogram D: Jean Yarborough
CAST: Frankie Darro (Frankie), Marcia Mae Jones, Jackie Moran, Keye Luke, Mantan Moreland, Gale Storm, Frank Sully, Barton Yarborough.

JUNIOR G-MEN OF THE AIR (1942)
Universal-Serial D: Ray Taylor and Lewis D. Collins
CAST: Billy Halop, Huntz Hall, Bernard Punsley, Gene Reynolds, Lionel Atwill, Frank Albertson, Richard Lane, Frankie Darro (Jack), David Gorcey.

JUNIOR PROM (1946)
Monogram D: Arthur Dreifuss
CAST: Freddie Stewart, June Preisser, Noel Neil, Jackie Moran, Warren Mills, Frankie Darro (Roy), Judy Clark, Murray Davis, Sam Flint.

FREDDIE STEPS OUT (1946)
Monogram D: Arthur Dreifuss
CAST: Freddie Stewart, June Preisser, Jackie Moran, Noel Neill, Ann Rooney, Warren Mills, Frankie Darro (Roy), Murray Davis, Milton Kibbee.

CHICK CARTER, DETECTIVE (1946)
Columbia Pictures-Serial D: Derwin Abrahams
CAST: Lyle Talbot, Douglas Fowley, Julie Gibson, Pamela Blake, Frankie Darro (Creeper).

HIGH SCHOOL HERO (1946)
Monogram D: Arthur Dreiifuss
CAST: Freddie Stewart, June Preisser, Noel Neill, Jackie Moran, Warren Mills, Frankie Darro (Roy), Ann Rooney, Milton Kibbee, Douglas Fowley.

VACATION DAYS (1947)
Monogram D: Arthur Dreifuss
CAST: Freddie Stewart, June Preisser, Frankie Darro (Roy), Warren Mills, Noel Neill, John Hart.

SARGE GOES TO COLLEGE (1947)
Monogram D: Will Jason
CAST: Freddie Stewart, June Preisser, Frankie Darro (Roy), Noel Neill, Arthur Walsh, Alan Hale,Jr.

THAT'S MY MAN (1947)
Republic Pictures D: Frank Borzage

CAST: Don Ameche, Catherine McLeod, Roscoe Karns, Joe Frisco, Gregory Marshall, Dorothy Adams, Frankie Darro (Daniels).

SMART POLITICS (1948)
Monogram D: Will Jason
CAST: Freddie Stewart, June Preisser, Frankie Darro (Roy), Warren Mills, Noel Neill, Donald McBride, Martha Davis, Butch Stone.

THE BABE RUTH STORY (1948)
Monogram D: Roy Del Rurh
CAST: William Bendix, Claire Trevor, Charles Bickford, Sam Levene, William Frawley, Stanley Clements, Frankie Darro (Newsboy).

HEART OF VIRGINIA (1948)
Republic Pictures D: R.G. Springsteen
CAST: Robert Lowery, Janet Martin, Frankie Darro (Jimmy Easter), Sam McDonald, Tom Chatterton, Bennie Bartlett, Glen Vernon, Edmond Cobb.

ANGEL'S ALLEY (1948)
Monogram D: William Beaudine CAST: Leo Gorcey, Huntz Hall, Billy Benedict, David Gorcey, Nestor Paiva, Frankie Darro (Jimmy), Gabriel Dell, Rosemary LaPlache.

TROUBLE MAKERS (1948)
Monogram D: Reginald LeBorg
CAST: Leo Gorcey, Huntz Hall, Billy Benedict, Frankie Darro (Feathers, also Leo Gorcey's stunt double), Gabriel Dell, Helen Parrish, Bernard Gorcey, John Ridgely, Lionel Stander.

HOLD THAT BABY (1949)
Monogram D: Reginald LeBorg
CAST: Leo Gorcey, Huntz Hall, Billy Benedict, Frankie Darro (Bananas), Anabel Shaw, Gabriel Dell, Bernard Gorcey, Bennie Bartlett.

FIGHTING FOOLS (1949)
Monogram D: Reginald LeBorg
CAST: Leo Gorcey, Huntz Hall, Billy Benedict, Frankie Darro
(Johnny Higgins), Gabriel Dell, Lyle Talbot, Bernard Gorcey, Bennie
Bartlett.

RIDING HIGH (1950)
Paramount D: Frank Capra
CAST: Bing Crosby, Collen Gray, Charles Bickford, Frances Gifford,
William Demarest, Raymond Walburn, Frankie Darro (Williams).

WYOMING MAIL (1950)
Universal D: Reginald LeBorg
CAST: Stephen McNally, Alexis Smith, Roy Roberts, Howard
DeSilva, Ed Begley, Dan Riss, Frankie Darro (Rafe).

SONS OF NEW MEXICO (1950)
Columbia D: John English
CAST: Gene Autry, Gail Davis, Robert Armstrong, Dick Jones,
Frankie Darro (Gig Jackson), Irving Jackson, Russell Arms.

A LIFE OF HER OWN (1950)
MGM D: George Cukor
CAST: Lana Turner, Ray Milland, Tom Ewell, Louis Calhern, Ann
Dovrak, Frankie Darro (Bellboy).

THE NEXT VOICE YOU HERE (1950)
MGM D: William A. Wellman
CAST: James Whitmore, Nancy Davis, Gary Grey, Lillian Bronson,
Art Smith, Tom D'Andrea, Frankie Darro (Silent bit part).

ACROSS THE WIDE MISSOURI (1951)
MGM D: William A. Wellman
CAST: Clark Gable, Ricardo Montalban, John Hodiak, Adolph
Menjou, Maria Elena Marques, J. Carroll Nash, Jack Holt, Frankie
Darro (Cadet).

THE PRIDE OF THE MARYLAND (1951)
Republic Pictures D: Phillip Ford
CAST: Stanley Clements, Peggy Stewart, Frankie Darro (Steve Lomis), Joe Sawyer, Robert Barrat, Harry Shannon.

WESTWARD THE WOMEN (1951)
MGM D: William A. Wellman
CAST: Robert Taylor, Denise Darcel, Henry Nakamura, Lenore Lonergan, Marilyn Erskine, Hope Emerson, Julie Bishop, Frankie Darro (Jean's Groom).

THE SELLOUT (1952)
MGM D: Gerald Mayer
CAST: Walter Pigeon, John Hodiak, Audrey Totter, Paula Raymond, Thomas Gomez, Cameron Mitchell, Karl Malden, Frankie Darro (Little Jake).

PAT AND MIKE (1952)
MGM D: George Cukor
CAST: Spencer Tracy, Katharine Hepburn, Aldo Ray, William Ching, Sammy White, Frankie Darro (Caddy).

SIREN OF BAGDAD (1953)
Columbia D: Richard Quine
CAST: Paul Henreid, Patricia Medina, Hans Conried, Charlie Lung, Laurette Luez, Anne Dore, Frankie Darro (Performer).

RACING BLOOD (1954)
20th Century Fox D: Wesley Barry
CAST: Bill Williams, Jean Porter, Jimmy Boyd, George Cleveland, John Eldredge, Sam Flint, Frankie Darro (Ben).

THE LAWLESS RIDER (1954)
United Artists D: Yakima Canutt
CAST: John Carpenter, Rose Bascom, Frankie Darro (Jim Bascom), Douglass Dumbrille, Frank Carpenter, Noel Neill, Kenne Duncan.

LIVING IT UP (1954)
Paramount D: Norman Taurog
CAST: Dean Martin, Jerry Lewis, Janet Leigh, Edward Arnold, Fred Clark, Frankie Darro (Bellboy).

TWO GUN MARSHALL (1955)
Allied Artists D: Frank McDonald
CAST: Guy Madison, Andy Devine, Raymond Hatton, Sara Haden, Carol Mathews, Frankie Darro (Clint Slocum). Feature version of the TV show "Adventures of Wild Bill Hickok."

THE TEN COMMANDMENTS (1956)
Paramount D: Cecil B. DeMille
CAST: Charlton Heston, Yul Brynner, Anne Baxter, Edward G. Robinson, Yvonne De Carlo, Debra Paget, Frankie Darro (Slave).

FORBIDDEN PLANET (1956)
MGM D: Fred McLeod
CAST: Walter Pidgeon, Anne Francis, Leslie Nielsen, Warren Stevens, Frankie Darro (Robbie the Robot).

TIP ON A DEAD JOCKEY (1957)
MGM D: Richard Thorpe
CAST: Robert Taylor, Dorothy Malone, Marcel Dalio, Martin Gabel, Frankie Darro (Jockey).

THE PERFECT FURLOUGH (1958)
Universal D: Blake Edwards
CAST: Tony Curtis, Janet Leigh, Keenan Wynn, Linda Cristal, Elaine Stritch, Marcel Dalio, Les Tremayne, Jay Novello, Frankie Darro (Man in cast).

OPERATION PETTICOAT (1959)
Universal D: Blake Edwards
CAST: Cary Grant, Tony Curtis, Joan O'Brien, Dina Merrill, Gene Evans, Arthur O'Connell, Richard Sargent, Virginia Gregg, Frankie Darro (Dooley).

DARBY O'GILL AND THE LITTLE PEOPLE (1959)
Disney D: Robert Stevensen
CAST: Albert Sharpe, Janet Munro, Sean Connery, Jimmy O'Dea,
Frankie Darro (Stunts).

THE GUN OF ZANGARA (1960)
Paramount D: Howard W. Koch
CAST: Robert Stack, Joe Mantell, Robert Middleton, Claude Akins,
Robert Anderson, Frankie Darro (News Vendor). Feature version of
the TV show "The Untouchables".

THE NOTORIOUS LANDLADY (1962)
Columbia D: Richard Quine
CAST: Kim Novak, Jack Lemmon, Fred Astaire,
Lionel Jeffries, Frankie Darro (Stunts).

THE CARPETBAGGERS (1964)
Paramount D: Edward Dmytryk
CAST: Alan Ladd, Carroll Baker, Bob Cummings, Martha Hyer, Lew
Ayres, Elizabeth Ashley, Martin Balsam, Frankie Darro (Porter).

THE DISORDERLY ORDERLY (1964)
Paramount D: Frank Tashlin
CAST: Jerry Lewis, Glenda Farrell, Everett Sloane, Karen Sharpe, Del
Moore, Frankie Darro (Board Member).

HOOK LINE AND SINKER (1969)
D: George Marshall
CAST: Jerry Lewis, Peter Lawford, Anne Francis, Pedro Gonzales-
Gonzales, Jimmy Miller, Frankie Darro (Delivery man).

FUGITIVE LOVERS (1975)
American Motion Pictures D: John Carr
CAST: Steve Oliver, Sondra Currie, Virginia Mayo, John Russell,
Goger Galloway, Vincent Barbi, Frankie Darro (Lester, the town
drunk).

SHORTS

Frankie appeared as himself in the following shorts:

SCREEN SNAPSHOTS-Series 9 No.22 (1930)

HOLLYWOOD ON PARADE (1932)

HOLLYWOOD ON PARADE-No. A-3 (1932)

SUNKIST STARS AT PALM SPRINGS (1936)

SCREEN SNAPSHOTS-Series 18 No.4 (1938)

TV SHOWS

THE ADVENTURES OF WILD BILL HICKOK (1951)
Ep: "The Slocum Family."

THE ALAN YOUNG SHOW (1952)

THE PUBLIC DEFENDER (1954)
Eps: "The Big Race" "Badge of Honor" "Cornered."

THE CHILDREN'S HOUR (1950's)
Ep: "The little People."

THE RED SKELTON SHOW (1955-70)
Frankie appeared on various shows throughout the early run of the show.

JUDGE ROY BEAN (1956)
Eps: "The Cross Draw Kid" "The Refugee."

THE LINE UP (1958)
Ep: "Gremlin Grady Case."

PETER GUNN (1958)
Ep: "The Jockey."

BAT MASTERSON (1959)
Ep: "Garrison Finish."

DECEMBER BRIDE (1958)
Ep: "The Ed Wynn Show."

HAVE GUN WILL TRAVEL (1958)
Ep: "The Last Laugh."

PERRY MASON (1958)
Ep: "The Case of the Terrified Typist."

THE FURTHER ADVENTURES OF ELLERY QUEEN (1959)
Ep: "Chauffeur Disguise."

ALFRED HITCHCOCK PRESENTS (1960)
Ep: "I Can Take Care of Myself."

CHECKMATE (1960)
Ep: "Death Runs Wild."

THE UNTOUCHABLES (1960)
Ep: "The Unhired Assassin."

MR. LUCKY (1960)
Ep: "Big Squeeze."

THE BIG BAFFLE (1961)
Ep: "Case of the Dangerous Robin."

THE HATHAWAYS (1961 or 1962)
Ep: "Charlie Goes to the Races."

GOING MY WAY (1962)
Ep: "Mr. Second Chance."

KEYHOLE (1962)
Ep: "The Cheaters."

ALFRED HITCHCOCK PRESENTS (1962)
Ep: "Ten O'Clock Tiger."

MISTER ED (1962)
Ep: "The Pilgrim."

BOB NEWHART SHOW (1962)

PERRY MASON (1964)
Ep: "The Case of the Ruinous Typist."

THE ADDAMS FAMILY (1965)
Ep: "Cousin It's Problem."

BATMAN (1966)
Eps: "Death Worse Than Fate" "Zelda the Great."

THE GUNS OF WILL SONNETT (1967)
Ep: "Find a Sonnett, Kill a Sonnett."

THE GIRL ON THE LATE LATE SHOW (1974)
TV Movie

BIBLIOGRAPHY

Books

Aylesworth, Thomas G. *Hollywood Kids.* New York: E.P. Dutton, 1987.

Brooks, Tim and Marsh, Earle. *The Complete Directory to Prime Time Network and Cable*
TV Shows 1946-Present. New York: Ballantine Books, 1995.

Cary, Diana Serra. *Hollywood's Children.* Dallas: Southern Methodist University Press,
1997.

Cary, Diana Serra. *What Ever Happened to Baby Peggy.* New York: St. Martin's Press, 1996.

Cary, Diana Serra. *Jackie Coogan: The World's Boy King.* Lanham, Maryland and Oxford: The Scarecrow Press, Inc., 2003.

Clarke, Gerald. *Get Happy.* New York: Random House, 2000

Coghlan, Frank "Junior", *They Still Call Me Junior.* Jefferson, North Carolina and London: McFarland, 1993.

Cocchi, John. *Second Feature.* New York: Carol Publishing Group, 1991.

Conway, Michael & Ricci, Mark. *The Films of Jean Harlow.* New York: Cadillac Publishing Co., Inc.,1965.

Conway, Michael and McGregor, Dion and Ricci, Mark. *The Films of Greta Garbo.* New York: Cadillac Publishing Co., Inc.,

Dickens, Homer. *The Films of James Cagney.* New Jersey: The Citadel Press, 1972.

Doherty, Thomas. *Pre-Code Hollywood.* New York: Columbia University Press, 1999.

Drake, Oliver. *Written Produced and Directed by Oliver Drake.* Mississippi: The Outlaw Press, Inc., 1990.

Fernett, Gene. *Hollywood's Poverty Row.* Florida: Coral Reef Publications, Inc., 1973.

Harmon, Jim and Glut, Donald F.. *The Great Movie Serials.* New York: Doubleday & Company, Inc., 1972.

Jewell, Richard B. with Harbin, Vernon. *The RKO Story.* New York: Arlington House. A Division of Crown Publishers, Inc.,1982.

Kinnard, Roy. *Science Fiction Serials.* Jefferson, North Carolina, and London: McFarland & Company, Inc., Publishers, 1998.

Lamparski, Richard. *Lamparski's Hidden Hollywood.* New York: Simon and Schuster A Division of Gulf & Western Corporation, 1981.

Lamparski, Richard. *Whatever Became of ...?* New York: Crown Publishers, Inc., 1973.

McCarthy, Todd and Flynn, Charles. *Kings of the Bs.* New York: E.P. Dutton & Co., Inc., 1975.

Munter, Pam. *When Teens Were Keen.* Los Angeles Colorado: Nicholas Lawrence Books. 2005.

Nareau, Bob. *Kid Kowboys.* North Carolina: Empire Publishing, Inc., 2003.

Okuda, Ted. *The Monogram Checklist* . Jefferson, North Carolina, and London: McFarland & Company, Inc., Publishers, 1987.

Pitts, Michael R. *Poverty Row Studios, 1929-1940.* Jefferson, North Carolina, and London: McFarland & Company, Inc., Publishers, 1997.

Price, Michael H. and Turner, George E.. *Forgotten Horrors 2.* Maryland: Midnight Marquee Press, 2001.

Price, Michael H. and Wooley, John with Turner, George E.. *Forgotten Horrors 3!* . Maryland: Luminary Press, 2003.

Quirk, Lawrence J.. *The Kennedys in Hollywood.* New York: Cooper Square Press, 2004.

Ringgold, Gene. *The Films of Bette Davis.* New York: Cadillac Publishing Co., Inc., MCMXLVI.

Sackett, Susan. *The Hollywood Reporter Book of Box Office Hits.* New York: Billboard Books, 1996.

Turner, George E. and Price, Michael H. *Forgotten Horrors.* Maryland: Midnight Marquee Press, Inc., 1999.

Tuska, Jon. *The Vanishing Legion.* Jefferson, North Carolina, and London: McFarland & Company, Inc., Publishers, 1982.

Vahimagi, Tise. *The Untouchables.* London: The British Film Institute, 1998.

Walker, Joseph and Walker, Juanita. *The Light On Her Face.* The
    ASC Press, 1984.
Warren, Bill. *Keep Watching the Skies!.* Jefferson & London:
    McFarland, 1982.
Weaver, Tom. *They Fought in the Creature Features.* Jefferson, North
    Carolina, and London: McFarland & Company, Inc., Publishers,
    1995.

Magazines

Photoplay-July 1928.
Shado Play-May 1934.
Picture Play-March *1935.*
TV Life-June 1957.
American Cinematographer-June 1993.
Mad About Movies-Summer 2000.
Video Watchdog-November 2004.